PROPERTY AND PROPHETS

the evolution of economic institutions and ideologies

E. K. Hunt
UNIVERSITY OF CALIFORNIA, RIVERSIDE

HARPER & ROW, PUBLISHERS
New York Evanston San Francisco London

TO MY MOTHER

PROPERTY AND PROPHETS
the evolution of economic
institutions and ideologies

 For information address Harper & Row, Publishers, Inc., 49 East 33rd Street, New York, N.Y. 10016.

Standard book number: 06–043018–4

Library of congress catalog card number: 74–184940

contents

preface

This book combines a brief review of the evolution of some of the most important institutions of capitalism with analyses of recurring ideological defenses of capitalism and radical critiques of capitalism. The unique feature of the book is the method of interweaving economic history and intellectual, or ideological, history. It is my belief that neither conservative defenses of capitalism nor radical rejections of it can be adequately appreciated until one is aware of the existential context within which they arose. This book attempts to provide an introduction to the study of the relationship between economic history and intellectual history.

No methodological arguments about the nature and extent of direct causal relations between economic history and intellectual history are made. Rather, I have merely juxtaposed events and ideas in a manner which I hope will stimulate the reader to ponder these issues and formulate his own conclusions.

My deep and lasting appreciation goes to all who have taught me, particularly Professors Sydney Coontz, Kiyotoshi Iwamoto, and Lawrence Nabers. Professor Howard J. Sherman has given me continuous friendship and encouragement in addition to providing extensive suggestions and criticisms which have improved the book. I am also grateful to Professors William Davisson, Douglas F. Dowd, Lynn Turgeon, Thomas Weisskopf, and Stephen T. Worland, each of whom read the manuscript in its entirety and made many valuable suggestions and criticisms. Finally, my gratitude and affection go to Audrey Wells for her help in preparing the manuscript.

E. K. Hunt

PROPERTY AND PROPHETS

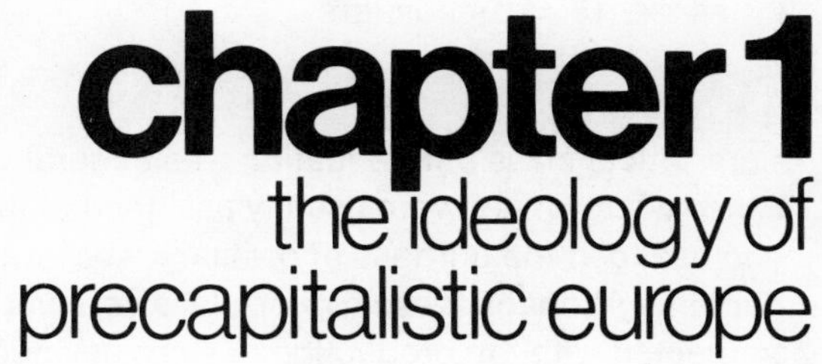

chapter 1
the ideology of precapitalistic europe

Human beings must exist in societies in order to survive. Unlike some species of animals, whose individual members can exist fairly adequately in relative isolation, human beings are not equipped by nature with the physical prowess individually to provide the material requisites of life. Humans survive and indeed prosper because by living in groups, they have learned to subdivide tasks and use tools. It was this division of labor and the accumulation of more and better tools (or capital) that made possible the impressive increases in man's control over nature, or increases in man's potential to produce the material necessities of life.

This division of labor also resulted, of necessity, in a differentiation of the roles that the different members of a society occupy. This differentiation was probably purely functional in earliest times; that is, when productivity was low, all members of a society lived near the subsistence level and social class, or hierarchical, differentiation was absent. Increasingly elaborate divisions of tasks, combined with more sophisticated tools, however, led to higher productivity which made possible the escape from the drudgery of everyday toil for at least a small part of society.

A small leisure class could be supported because with higher per capita productivity, the labor of a smaller number of persons could support the entire society at its customary standard of living or at an even higher standard. When this occurred, societies began to differentiate among their members according to social class. This hierarchical class differentiation was generally economic in nature. Those who worked were usually assigned to the lowest classes; those who escaped the burdens of ordinary labor were of higher class standing. Although these higher-class persons no longer were directly connected with the production of everyday necessities, they often performed rites, rituals, or extensive duties, some of which were undoubtedly beneficial to the society.

As human productive and social relations became more complex, an economic system evolved. An *economic system* is a set of principles, laws, or customs by which society assures itself that persons with appropriate skills are available to perform the necessary productive tasks at the proper place and time. The economic system also provides a mechanism to allocate properly the produced goods and services among the different social classes. Moreover, the system determines the size of the shares going to different persons within the various classes.

Such a system could not continue to exist for long if the majority of its members did not share common feelings about the proper way of conducting economic and social affairs. These common feelings and values, which generally stemmed from a common world view, or system of metaphysics, justified both the division of productive tasks and the class differentiation that existed. These common feelings and values were expressed in ideologies.

An *ideology,* as the term is used in this book, refers to those ideas and beliefs that tend to justify morally a society's social and economic relationships. Most members of a society internalize the ideology and thus believe that their functional role as well as the functional roles of others are morally correct and that the method by which society divides its produce is fair. This common belief gives society its cohesiveness and viability. Lack of it creates turmoil and strife—and ultimately revolution, if the differences are deep enough!

This book is primarily concerned with our present economic system: capitalism. We sketch the broad outlines of the evolution of this system. In doing so, we focus on conflicts and social antagonisms and examine the ideologies with which the capitalist system attempted to mitigate these conflicts and to promote social cohesiveness.

From its beginning, the capitalist system created a large class of rebels, dreamers, and visionaries who rejected it. They mentally constructed utopian schemes of how a good society should be organized and used these schemes as the basis for moral attacks on the excesses and suffering they saw in the capitalist system. Throughout most of its history, the socialist movement was no more than anticapitalist ideas, writings, propaganda, and agitation. Only in the twentieth century has the term *socialism* been used to describe an actual, existing economy.

Throughout most of this book, we shall be concerned with the economic, social, and ethical views that have been used either to defend or to attack capitalism. By way of background, we shall first examine the code of ethics that can be traced from its biblical Judeo-Christian origins to its zenith in medieval feudal society. Feudal society was the social and economic system from which capitalism evolved. The Judeo-Christian tradition, which was the basis of medieval ideology, proved to be incompatible with many of the institutions and practices necessary for the maintenance of capitalism. This conflict of the traditional religious and moral code with the emerging economic and social system, and the ways in which men sought to resolve this conflict, provides a framework that is helpful in understanding the later critiques and defenses of capitalism.

Men who sought to provide an intellectual defense for the new capitalist system proceeded along two separate paths. Some tried to modify and alter certain key elements of the Judeo-Christian ethic. Others abandoned that ethical and philosophical tradition completely and embraced a new philosophical world view compatible with capitalism. The conflicts between these two basic types of capitalist ideologies will be explored in later chapters.

There was still another way of reconciling the conflict between the Judeo-Christian ethical tradition and the emerging capitalist system. One could reject the institutions and practices of capitalism that conflicted with the ethical tradition. This course of thought gave impetus to the socialist movement, and certain elements of the Judeo-Christian ethic had (and still have) a very important influence in the formation of socialist as well as capitalist ideologies.

the christian corporate ethic

The Judeo-Christian moral code will be called the *Christian corporate ethic* in this book. It can be understood most easily by comparing society with a family. Those with positions of power and wealth can be likened to the father or keeper of the family. They have strong paternalistic obligations toward the common people, the poor, or in our analogy, the children. The common man, however, is expected to accept his place in the society and to subordinate himself willingly to the leadership of the wealthy and the powerful in much the same way that a child accepts the authority of his father.

The Old Testament Jews[1] quite literally regarded themselves as the children of one God. This relationship meant that all Jews were

[1] This account relies on Alexander Gray, *The Socialist Tradition* (London: Longmans, 1963), chap. 2.

brothers; the Mosaic law was intended to maintain this feeling of membership in one big family. This brotherhood was one of grown children who acknowledged their mutual obligations, even though they no longer shared possessions.

From the confused mass of duties and regulations governing the early Jews, the most salient feature is the large number of provisions made for the prevention and relief of poverty. Their humane treatment of debtors was also notable. Each Jew was to be his brother's keeper; indeed, the obligations extended to caring for his neighbor's animals should they wander his way.[2] The first duty of all, however, and even more particularly of the wealthy, was the caring for the poor: "Thou shalt open thine hand wide unto thy brother, to the poor, and to the needy, in the land."[3] An important element in this paternalistic code was the sanction against taking a worker's tools as a means of satisfying a debt: "No man shall take the nether or the upper millstone to pledge: for he taketh a man's life to pledge."[4] The same point was made elsewhere in the Old Testament: "He that taketh away his neighbor's living slayeth him."[5]

All Jews did not, of course, live up to these lofty professions. Great extremes of wealth and poverty existed that would have been impossible had the Mosaic law been strictly observed. Many of the prophets, who were often radical champions of the poor, eloquently denounced the rich for their abuse of their wealth, for their wicked, slothful luxury and general unrighteousness. The important point is not that they failed to live up to the code, but that the moral code of this small tribe left so important an imprint on much of subsequent history.

The teachings of Christ in the New Testament carry on part of the Mosaic tradition relevant to economic ideology. He taught the necessity of being concerned with the welfare of one's brother, the importance of charity and almsgiving, and the evil of selfish acquisitiveness and covetousness. His emphasis on the special responsibilities and obligations of the rich is even more pronounced than that of the earlier Jewish writers. In fact, on the basis of a reading of the Gospel of Luke, one might conclude that Christ condemned the rich simply because they were rich and praised the poor simply because they were poor: "Woe unto you that are rich! . . . Woe unto you that are full! for ye shall hunger. Woe unto you that laugh now! for ye shall mourn and weep."[6] However, on

[2] Deut., 22:1–4.

[3] Deut., 15:7–11.

[4] Deut., 24:6.

[5] Eccles., 34:22.

[6] Quoted in Gray, op. cit., p. 41.

examining the other Gospels, it must be concluded, that this probably is Luke speaking, not Christ. Luke must be seen as the radical "leveller among the apostles."[7]

In the other Gospels, there are warnings that wealth may be a stumbling block in getting to heaven, but there is no condemnation of wealth as such. The most important passages in this regard deal with the wealthy young man who wants to know what he must do to attain eternal life.[8] Christ's first answer amounts to nothing more than a brief statement of the Ten Commandments. It is only after being pressed further that Christ goes beyond the binding, universal moral requirements to a counsel of perfection. "If thou wilt be perfect"[9] begins the statement in which he tells the young man to sell whatever he has and give to the poor.

The Christian corporate ethic, with its paternalistic obligations of the wealthy toward the poor, was developed more specifically and elaborately by most of the later Christian fathers. The writings of Clement of Alexandria are a reasonably good reflection of the traditional attitudes of the early church. He emphasized the dangers of greed, love of material things, and acquiring of wealth. Those who had wealth were under a special obligation to treat it as a gift of God and to use it wisely in the promotion of the general well-being of others.

Clement's *The Rich Man's Salvation* was written in order to free the rich of the "unfounded despair" they might have acquired from reading passages in the Gospels, such as those found in Luke. Clement began by asserting that contrary to anything one might find in Luke, "it is no great or enviable thing to be simply without riches." Those who were poor would not for that reason alone find God's blessedness. In order to seek salvation, the rich man need not renounce his wealth, but need merely "banish from the soul its opinions about riches, its attachment to them, its excessive desire, its morbid excitement over them, its anxious cares, the thorns of our earthly existence which choke the seed of the true life."[10]

Not the possession of wealth, but the way in which it was used was important to Clement. The wealthy were given the responsibility of administering their wealth, on God's behalf, to alleviate the suffering and promote the general welfare of their brothers. In decreeing that the hungry should be fed and the naked should be clothed, God certainly had not willed a situation in which no one could carry out these commandments for lack of sufficient material prerequisites.

[7] Ibid., p. 42.

[8] Matt., 19:16–26; Mark, 10:17–27; Luke, 18.

[9] Matt., 19.

[10] Quoted in Gray, op. cit., p. 48.

It followed, thus, that God had willed that some men should have wealth, but had given them the important function of paternalistically caring for the well-being of the rest of society.

In a similar vein, Ambrose wrote that "riches themselves are not blamable" as long as they are used righteously. In order to use wealth righteously, "we ought to be of mutual help one to the other, and to vie with each other in doing duties, to lay all our advantages . . . before all, and . . . to bring help one to the other."[11]

The list of Christian fathers who wrote lengthy passages to the same effect could be expanded greatly. Suffice it to say that by the early feudal period, the Christian corporate ethic was thoroughly entrenched in western European culture. Greed, avarice, materialistic self-seeking, the desire to accumulate wealth—all such individualistic and materialistic motives—were sharply condemned. The acquisitive, individualistic person was considered the very antithesis of the good man, who concerned himself with the well-being of all his brothers. The wealthy man had the potential to do either great good or great evil with his wealth and power, and the worst evil resulted when wealth was used either exclusively for self-gratification or as a means of continually acquiring more wealth for its own sake. The righteously wealthy were those who realized that their wealth and power were God's gift, that they were morally obligated to act as paternalistic stewards, and that they were to administrate worldly affairs in order to promote the welfare of all.

This Christian corporate ethic reached its zenith during the feudal period of European history. Because the feudal manorial system was the social and economic system that immediately preceded capitalism, the evolution of capitalism can best be understood if the feudal manorial society and its Christian ideology are examined first.

feudalism

The decline of the western part of the old Roman Empire left Europe without the laws and protection that the empire had provided. The vacuum was filled by the creation of a feudal hierarchy. In this hierarchy, the serf, or peasant, was protected by the lord of the manor, who in turn owed allegiance to and was protected by an overlord, who himself owed allegiance to and was protected by a higher overlord. And so the system went, ending eventually with the king. The strong protected the weak, but they did so at a high price. In return for payments of money, food, labor, or military allegiance,

[11] Ibid., p. 49.

overlords granted the fief, or feudum—a hereditary right to use land—to their vassals. At the bottom was the serf, a peasant who tilled the land. The vast majority of the population raised crops for food or clothing or tended sheep for wool and clothing.[12]

Custom and tradition are the key to understanding medieval relationships. In place of laws as we know them today, the *custom of the manor* governed. There was no strong central authority in the Middle Ages that could have enforced a system of laws. The entire medieval organization was based on a system of mutual obligations and services up and down the hierarchy. Possession or use of the land obligated one to certain customary services or payments in return for protection. The lord was as obligated to protect the serf as the serf was to turn over a portion of his crop to or perform extensive labor for the lord.

Customs were broken, of course; no system always operates in fact as it is designed to operate in theory. One should not, however, underestimate the strength of custom and tradition in determining the lives and ideas of medieval people. Disputes between serfs were decided in the lords' courts according to both the special circumstances of each case and the general customs of the manor for such cases. Of course, a dispute between a serf and a lord would usually be decided in his own favor by the lord. Even in this circumstance, however, especially in England, an overlord would impose sanctions or punishments on a lord who, as his vassal, had persistently violated the customs in his treatment of serfs. This rule by the custom of the manor stands in sharp contrast to the legal and judicial system of capitalism. The capitalist system is based on the enforcement of contracts and universally binding laws, which are only rarely softened by the possible mitigating circumstances and customs that often swayed the lord's judgment in medieval times.

The extent to which the lords could enforce their "rights" varied greatly from time to time and from place to place. It was the strengthening of these obligations and the nobleman's ability to enforce them through a long hierarchy of vassals and over a wide area, that eventually led to the emergence of the modern nation-states. This process occurred during the period of transition from feudalism to capitalism. Throughout most of the Middle Ages, however, many of the claims were very weak because political control was very fragmented.

The basic economic institution of medieval rural life was the manor, which contained within it two separate and distinct classes: noble-

[12] For a more complete discussion of the medieval economic and social system, see J. H. Claphan and Eileen E. Power, eds., *The Agrarian Life of the Middle Ages*, 2nd ed, The Cambridge Economic History of Europe, vol. I (London: Cambridge University Press, 1966).

men, or lords of the manors, and the serfs (from the Latin word *servus,* or "slave"). Serfs were not really slaves. Unlike a slave, who was simply property to be bought and sold at will, the serf could not be parted from either his family or his land. If his lord transferred possession of the manor to another nobleman, the serf simply had another lord. In varying degrees, however, obligations were placed upon the serfs that were sometimes very onerous and from which there was often no escape. Usually, they were far from being "free."

The lord lived off the labor of the serfs who farmed his fields and paid taxes in kind and money according to the custom of the manor. Similarly, the lord gave protection, supervision, and administration of justice according to the custom of the manor. It must be added that although the system did rest on reciprocal obligations, the concentration of economic and political power in the hands of the lord led to a system in which, by any standard, the serf was exploited in the extreme.

The Catholic church was by far the largest owner of land during the Middle Ages. While bishops and abbots occupied much the same place as counts and dukes in the feudal hierarchy, there was one important difference between the religious and the secular lords. Dukes and counts might shift their loyalty from one overlord to another (depending on the circumstances and the balance of power involved), but the bishops and abbots always had (in principle at least) a primary loyalty to the church in Rome. This was also an age during which the religious teaching of the church had a very strong and pervasive influence throughout western Europe. These factors combined to make the church the closest thing to a strong, central government throughout this period.

Thus, the manor might be secular or religious (many times secular lords had religious overlords and vice versa), but the essential relationships between the lords and the serfs were not significantly affected by this distinction. There is little evidence that serfs were treated any less harshly by religious lords than by secular lords. The church lords and the secular nobility were the joint ruling classes; they controlled the land and the power that went with it. In return for very onerous appropriations of the serfs' labor, produce, and money, the nobility provided military protection and the church provided spiritual aid.

In addition to manors, medieval Europe had many towns, which were important centers of manufacturing. Manufactured goods were sold to manors and, sometimes, were traded in long-distance commerce. The dominant economic institutions in the towns were the guilds—craft, professional, and trade associations that had existed as far back as the Roman Empire. If anyone wanted to produce or sell any good or service, he had to join a guild.

The guilds were as involved with social and religious as with economic questions. They regulated their members' conduct in all their activities: personal, social, religious, and economic. Although the guilds did regulate very carefully the production and sale of commodities, they were less concerned with making profits than with saving their members' souls. Salvation demanded that the individual lead an orderly life based upon church teachings and custom. Thus, the guilds exerted a powerful influence as conservators of the status quo in the medieval towns.

the anticapitalist nature of feudal ideology

The philosophical and religious assumptions upon which medieval people acted were extensions of the Christian corporate ethic. The many particular additions to the ethic were profoundly conservative in purpose and content. Both the continuity in and conservative modifications of the ethic can be seen in the writings of Thomas Aquinas, the preeminent spokesman of the Middle Ages.

Tradition was upheld in his insistence that private property could be justified *morally* only because it was a necessary condition for almsgiving. The rich, he asserted, must always be "ready to distribute, . . . [and] willing to communicate."[13] Aquinas believed, with the earlier fathers, that "the rich man, if he does not give alms, is a thief."[14] The rich man held wealth and power for God and for all society. He administered his wealth for God and for the common good of mankind. Without proper use and administration of this wealth, it could no longer be religiously and morally justified, in which case the wealthy man was to be considered a common thief.

Aquinas' and, indeed, most of the medieval church fathers' profoundly conservative addition to the Christian corporate ethic was their insistence that the economic and social relationships of the medieval manorial system reflected a natural and eternal ordering of these relationships. Indeed, these relationships were ordained by God. They stressed the importance of a division of labor and effort, with different tasks assigned to the different classes, and insisted that the social and economic distinctions between the classes were necessary to accommodate this specialization.

If one was in the position of a lord (secular or religious), it was necessary to have an abundance of material wealth in order to do

[13] Gray, op. cit., p. 57.

[14] Ibid.

well the tasks that providence had assigned. Of course, it took almost nothing to perform the tasks expected of a serf. It was every person's duty to labor unquestioningly at the task to which providence had assigned him, to accept the station into which he was born, and to accept the rights of others to have and do those things appropriate to their stations in life. Thus, despite its paternalism, the Christian corporate ethic could be used (and was used) to defend as natural and just the great inequities and intense exploitation that flowed from the concentration of wealth and power in the hands of the church and nobility.

Any account of medieval social and economic thought must also stress the great disdain with which they viewed trade and commerce and the commercial spirit. The medieval way of life was based upon custom and tradition; its viability depended upon the members of society accepting that tradition and their place within it. Where the capitalist commercial ethic prevails, greed, selfishness, covetousness, and the desire to better oneself materially or socially are accepted by most people as innate qualities. Yet they were uniformly denounced and reviled in the Middle Ages. The serfs (and, sometimes, the lower nobility) tended to be dissatisfied with the traditions and customs of medieval society, and thus threatened the stability of the feudal system. It is not surprising, therefore, to find pervasive moral sanctions designed to repress or to mitigate the effects of these motives.

One of the most important of such sanctions, which was repeated over and over throughout this period, was the insistence that it was the moral duty of merchants and traders to transact all trade or exchanges at the just price. This notion illustrates the role that paternalistic social control played in the feudal era. A *just price* was one that would compensate the seller for his efforts in transporting the good and in finding the buyer at a rate that was just sufficient to maintain the seller at his *customary* or *traditional* station in life. Prices above the just price would, of course, lead to profits, which would be accumulated as material wealth.

It was the lust for wealth that the Christian corporate ethic consistently condemned. Thus, the doctrine of the just price was intended as a curb on such acquisitive and socially disruptive behavior. Then as now, the accumulation of material wealth was a passport to greater power and upward social mobility. This social mobility was eventually to prove totally destructive of the medieval system because it put an end to the status relationships that were the backbone of medieval society.

Another example of this condemnation of acquisitive behavior was the prohibition on usury, or the loaning of money at interest. A "bill against usury" that was passed in England reflected the attitudes of most of the people of those times. It read in part:

> But forasmuch as usury is by the word of God utterly prohibited, as a vice most odious and detestable . . . which thing, by no godly teachings and persuasions can sink in to the hearts of divers greedy, uncharitable and covetous person of this Realm . . . be it enacted . . . that . . . no person or persons of what Estate, degree, quality or condition so ever he or they be, by any corrupt, colorable or deceitful conveyance, sleight or engine, or by any way or mean, shall lend, give, set out, deliver or forbear any sum or sums of money . . . to or for any manner of usury, increase, lucre, gain or interest to be had, received or hoped for, over and above the sum or sums so lent . . . as also of the usury . . . upon pain of imprisonment.[15]

The church believed that usury was the worst sort of acquisitive behavior because most loans upon which interest was charged were granted to poor farmers or peasants after a bad crop or some other tragedy had befallen them. Thus, interest was a gain made at the expense of one's brother at a time when he was most in need of help and charity. Of course, the Christian ethic strongly condemned such rapacious exploitation of a needy brother.

Many historians have pointed out that bishops and abbots as well as dukes, counts, and kings often flagrantly violated these sanctions. They themselves granted loans at interest, even while they were punishing others for doing so. We are more interested, however, in the values and motives of the period than in the sins and infractions of the rules. The values of the feudal system stand in stark, antithetical contrast to those that were shortly to prevail under a capitalist system. The desires to maximize monetary gain, to accumulate material wealth, and to advance oneself socially and economically through acquisitive behavior were to become the dominant motive forces in the capitalist system.

The sins that were most strongly denounced within the context of the Christian corporate ethic were to become the behavioral assumptions upon which the entire capitalist market economy was to be based. It is obvious that such a radical change would render the Christian corporate ethic, at least in its medieval version, inadequate as the basis of a moral justification of the new capitalist system. The ethic would have to be modified drastically or rejected completely in order to elaborate a defense for the new system. Attempts to do both are explored in subsequent chapters.

[15] Quoted in Leo Huberman, *Man's Worldly Goods* (New York: Monthly Review Press, 1961), p. 39.

summary

Economic systems organize human effort to transform the resources given in nature into usable articles, or economic goods. Ideologies are systems of ideas and beliefs that are used to justify morally the economic and social relationships within an economic system.

The Christian corporate ethic was used to justify the feudal economy and its attendant social and economic relationships. This ideology contained elements that were antithetical to the functioning of a capitalist market system. In later chapters, we shall examine the ways in which men attempted to substitute new ideologies for the older Christian corporate ethic or to modify this ethic in such a way that it could be used to provide a moral justification of a capitalist market economic system.

chapter 2
the transition to early capitalism and the beginnings of the mercantilist view

The medieval society was an agrarian society. The social hierarchy was based on individuals' ties to the land, and the entire social system rested on an agricultural base. Yet, ironically, increases in agricultural productivity were the original impetus to a series of profound changes. These changes, occurring over several centuries, resulted in the dissolution of medieval feudalism and the beginnings of capitalism.

changes in technology

The most important technological advance in the Middle Ages was the replacement of the two-field system of crop rotation with the three-field system. Although there is evidence that the three-field system was introduced into Europe as early as the eighth century, its use was probably not widespread until around the eleventh century.

Yearly sowing of the same land would deplete the land and eventually make it unusable. Consequently, in the two-field system, one-half of the land was always allowed to lie fallow in order to recover from the previous year's planting.

With the three-field system, arable land was divided into three equal fields. Rye or winter wheat would be planted in the fall in the first field. Oats, beans, or peas would be planted in the spring in the second field. The third field would lie fallow. In each subsequent year there was a rotation of these positions. Any given piece of land would have a fall planting one year, a spring planting the next year, and would lie fallow the third year.

A dramatic increase in agricultural output resulted from this seemingly simple change in agricultural technology. With the same amount of arable land, the three-field system could increase the amount under cultivation at any particular time by as much as 50 percent.[1]

The three-field system led to other important changes. Spring sowing of oats and other fodder crops enabled the people to support more horses, which began to replace oxen as the principal source of power in agriculture. Horses were much faster than oxen, and consequently, the region under cultivation could be extended. Larger cultivated areas enabled the countryside to support more concentrated population centers. Transportation of men, commodities, and equipment was much more efficient with horses. Greater efficiency was also attained in plowing: A team of oxen required three men to do the plowing; a horse-drawn plow could be operated by one man. The costs of transporting agricultural products was substantially reduced in the thirteenth century, when the four-wheeled wagon with a pivoted front axle replaced the two-wheeled cart.

These improvements in agriculture and transportation contributed to two important and far-reaching changes. First, they made possible a rapid increase in population growth. The best historical estimates show that the population of Europe doubled between 1000 and 1300.[2] Second, closely related to the expansion of population was a rapid increase in urban concentration. Prior to the year 1000, most of Europe, except for a few Mediterranean trade centers, consisted of only manors, villages, and a few small towns. By 1300, there were many thriving cities and larger towns.

The growth of towns and cities led to a growth of rural–urban specialization. With urban workers severing all ties to the soil, the output of manufactured goods increased impressively. Along with increased manufacturing and increased economic specialization came many additional gains in human productivity. Interregional, long-distance trade and commerce was also a very important result of this increased specialization.

1 Lynn White, Jr., *Medieval Technology and Social Change* (Oxford: Clarendon, 1962) pp. 71–72.

2 Harry A. Miskimin, *The Economy of Early Renaissance Europe, 1300–1460* (Englewood Cliffs, N.J.: Prentice-Hall, 1969) p. 20.

the increase in long-distance trade

The single most persistent force that led to the disintegration of medieval traditions and customs was the spread of trade and commerce. The expansion of trade, particularly long-distance trade in the early period, led to the establishment of commercial and industrial towns that serviced this trade. And the growth of these cities and towns, and their increased domination by merchant capitalists, led to important changes in both industry and agriculture. Each of these areas of change, particularly the latter, brought about a weakening and ultimately a complete dissolving of the traditional ties that held together the feudal economic and social structure.

From the earliest part of the medieval period, some long-distance trade had been carried on throughout many parts of Europe. This trade was very important in southern Europe, on the Mediterranean and Adriatic seas, and in northern Europe, on the North and Baltic seas. Between these two centers of commercialism, however, the feudal manorial system in most of the rest of Europe was relatively unaffected by commerce and trade until the later Middle Ages.

From about the eleventh century onward, the Christian Crusades in southern Europe and the piracy and commerce of the Vikings in northern Europe gave the impetus to a marked expansion of commerce from both directions. This development led to the great trade fairs that flourished from the twelfth through the late fourteenth centuries. Held annually in the principal European trading cities, these fairs usually lasted from one to several weeks. Northern European merchants exchanged their grain, fish, wool, cloth, timber, pitch, tar, salt, and iron for the spices, silks, brocades, wines, fruits, and gold and silver that were the dominant items in southern European commerce.[3]

By the fifteenth century, the fairs were being replaced by commercial cities where year-round markets thrived. The trade and commerce of these cities was incompatible with restrictive feudal customs and traditions. Generally, the cities were successful in gaining independence from church and feudal lords. Within these commercial centers there arose complex systems of currency exchange, debt-clearing, and credit facilities, and modern business instruments such as bills of exchange came into widespread use. New systems of *commercial law* developed. Unlike the system of

[3] For a more complete discussion of the rise of trade and commerce, see Dudley Dillard, *Economic Development of the North Atlantic Community* (Englewood Cliffs, N.J.: Prentice-Hall, 1967), pp. 3–178.

paternalistic adjudication based upon custom and tradition that prevailed in the manor, the commercial law was fixed by precise code. Hence, it became the basis of the modern capitalistic law of contracts, negotiable instruments, agency sales, and auctions.

In the manorial handicraft industry, the producer (the master craftsman) was also the seller. The industries that burgeoned in the new cities, however, were primarily export industries in which the producer was distant from the final buyer. Craftsmen sold their goods wholesale to merchants, who, in turn, transported and resold them. Another important difference was that the manorial craftsman was also generally a farmer. The new city craftsman gave up farming to devote himself to his craft, with which he obtained a money income that could be used to satisfy his other needs.

the putting-out system and the birth of capitalist industry

As trade and commerce thrived and expanded, the need for more manufactured goods and greater reliability of supply led to increasing control of the productive process by the merchant-capitalist. By the sixteenth century, the handicraft type of industry, in which the craftsman owned his workshop, tools, and raw materials and functioned as an independent, small-scale entrepreneur, had largely been replaced in the exporting industries by the putting-out system. In the earliest period of the *putting-out system,* the merchant-capitalist would furnish an independent craftsman with raw materials, and pay him a fee to work the materials into finished products. In this way, the capitalist owned the product throughout all stages of production, although the work was done in independent workshops. In the later period of the putting-out system, the merchant-capitalist owned the tools and machinery and often owned the building in which the production took place. He hired workers to use these tools, furnished them with the raw materials, and took the finished products.

The worker no longer sold a finished product to the merchant. Rather, he sold only his labor power. The textile industries were among the first in which the putting-out system developed. Weavers, spinners, fullers, and dyers found themselves in a situation where their employment, and hence their ability to support themselves and their families, depended upon the merchant-capitalists who had to sell what the workers produced at a price that was high enough to pay wages and other costs and still make a profit.

Capitalist control was, then, extended into the process of production. At the same time, a labor force was created that owned little or no capital and had nothing to sell but its labor power. These two features mark the appearance of the economic system of capitalism. Some writers and historians have defined capitalism as existing when trade, commerce, and the commercial spirit expanded and became more important in Europe. Trade and commerce, however, had existed throughout the feudal era. Yet as long as feudal tradition remained the organizing principle in production, trade and commerce were really outside the social and economic system. The market and the search for money profits replaced custom and tradition in determining who would perform what task, how the task would be performed, and whether a given worker could find work to support himself. When this occurred, the capitalist system was created.[4]

Capitalism became dominant with the extension to most lines of production of the relationship that existed between capitalists and workers in the sixteenth-century export industries. For such a system to evolve, the economic self-sufficiency of the feudal manor had to be broken down and manorial customs and traditions had to be undermined or destroyed. Agriculture had to become a capitalistic venture in which workers would sell their labor power to capitalists, and capitalists would buy labor only if they expected to make a profit in the process.

A capitalist textile industry existed in Flanders in the thirteenth century. When, for various reasons, its prosperity began to decline, the wealth and poverty it had created led to a long series of violent class wars, starting around 1280, that almost completely destroyed the industry. In the fourteenth century, a capitalist textile industry flourished in Florence. There, as in Flanders, adverse business conditions led to tensions between a poverty-stricken working class and their affluent capitalist employers. The results of these tensions were violent rebellions in 1379 and 1382. Failure to resolve these class antagonisms significantly worsened the precipitous decline in the Florentine textile industry, as it had done earlier in Flanders.

In the fifteenth century, England dominated the world textile market. Its capitalist textile industry solved the problem of class conflict by ruralizing the industry. Whereas the earlier capitalist textile industries of Flanders and Florence had been in the densely populated cities, where the workers were thrown together and organized resistance was easy to initiate, the English fulling mills were scattered about the countryside. This meant that the workers were isolated from all but a small handful of other workers, and effective organized resistance did not develop.

[4] See Maurice H. Dobb, *Studies in the Development of Capitalism* (London: Routledge & Kegan Paul, 1946), particularly chap. 4.

The later system, however, in which wealthy owners of capital employed propertyless craftsmen, was usually a phenomenon of the city rather than of the countryside. From the beginning, these capitalistic enterprises sought monopolistic positions from which to exploit the demand for their products. The rise of livery guilds, or associations of merchant-capitalist employers, created a host of barriers to protect their position. Different types of apprenticeships, with special privileges and exemptions for the sons of the wealthy, excessively high membership fees, and other barriers, prevented ambitious poorer craftsmen from competing with, or entering, the new capitalist class. Indeed, these barriers generally resulted in the transformation of poorer craftsmen and their sons into a new urban working class that lived exclusively by selling its labor power.

the decline of the manorial system

Before a complete system of capitalism could emerge, however, the force of capitalist market relations had to invade the rural manor, the bastion of feudalism. The vast increase of population in the new trading cities led to this penetration into the manor. Large urban populations depended upon the rural countryside for food and much of the raw materials for export industries. These needs fostered a rural–urban specialization and a large flow of trade between the rural manor and the city. The lords of the manors began to depend on the cities for manufactured goods and increasingly came to desire luxury goods that merchants could sell to them.

The peasants on the manor also found they could exchange surpluses for money at the local grain markets, which could be used by the peasants to purchase commutation of their labor services.[5] Commutation often resulted in a situation in which the peasant became very nearly an independent small businessman. He might rent the land from the lord, sell the produce to cover the rents, and retain the remaining revenues himself. This system gave peasants a higher incentive to produce and thereby increased their surplus marketings, which led to more commutations, more subsequent marketings, and so forth. The cumulative effect was a very gradual breaking down of the traditional ties of the manor and a substitution of the market and the search for profits as the organizing principle of production. By the middle of the fourteenth century, money rents in many parts of Europe exceeded the value of labor services.

Another force that brought the market into the countryside and

[5] Commutation involved the substitution of money rents for the labor services required of the serf.

that was closely related to commutation was the alienation of the lords' demesnes. The lords who needed cash to exchange for manufactured goods and luxuries began to rent their own lands to peasant farmers, rather than having them farmed directly with labor-service obligations. This process led increasingly to a situation in which the lord of the manor was simply a landlord in the modern sense of that term. In fact, he very often became an absentee landlord, as many lords chose to move to the cities or were away fighting battles.

The breakup of the manorial system, however, stemmed more directly from a series of catastrophies in the late fourteenth and fifteenth centuries. The Hundred Years' War between France and England (1337–1453) created general disorder and unrest in those countries. The Black Death was even more devastating. On the eve of the plague of 1348–1349, England's population stood at 4 million. By the early fifteenth century, after the effects of the wars and the plague, England had a scant 2.5-million population. This was fairly typical of trends in other European countries. The depopulation led to a desperate labor shortage, and wages for all types of labor rose abruptly. Land, now relatively more plentiful, began to rent for less.

These facts led the feudal nobility to attempt to revoke the commutations they had granted and to reestablish the labor-service obligations of the serfs and peasants (peasants were former serfs who had attained some degree of independence and freedom from feudal restrictions). They found, however, that the clock could not be turned back. The market had been extended into the countryside, and with it had come greater freedom, independence, and prosperity for the peasants. They bitterly resisted efforts to reinstate the old obligations. Their resistance did not go unchallenged.

The result was the famous peasant revolts that broke out all over Europe from the late fourteenth through the early sixteenth centuries. These rebellions were extreme in their cruelty and ferocity. A contemporary French writer described a band of peasants who killed a "knight and putting him on a broach, roasted him over a fire in the sight of his wife and children. Ten or twelve of them ravished the wife and then forced her to eat of her husband's flesh. Then they killed her and her children. Wherever these ungracious people went they destroyed good houses and strong castles."[6] Rebellious peasants were ultimately slaughtered with equal or greater cruelty and ferocity by the nobility.

England experienced a series of such revolts in the late fourteenth and fifteenth centuries. But the revolts that occurred in Germany in the early sixteenth century were probably the bloodiest of all. The

6 N. S. B. Gras, *A History of Agriculture in Europe and America* (New York: Appleton, 1940), p. 108.

peasant rebellion in 1524–1525 was crushed by the Imperial troops of the Holy Roman emperor, who slaughtered peasants by the tens of thousands. Over 100,000 persons probably were killed in Germany alone.

These revolts are mentioned here to illustrate the fact that fundamental changes in the economic and political structure of a social system are often achieved only after traumatic and violent social conflict. Any economic system generates a class or classes whose privileges are dependent on the continuation of that system. Quite naturally, these classes go to great lengths to resist change and to protect their positions. The feudal nobility fought a savage rearguard action against the emerging capitalist market system, but the forces of change ultimately swept them aside. Although the important changes were brought about by aspiring merchants and minor noblemen, the peasants were the pathetic victims of the consequent social upheavals. Ironically, the peasants were usually struggling to protect the status quo.

other forces in the transition to capitalism

The early sixteenth century is a watershed in European history. It vaguely marks the dividing line between the old, decaying feudal order and the rising capitalist system. After 1500, important social and economic changes began to occur with increasing frequency, each reinforcing the other, and together having the cumulative effect of ushering in the system of capitalism. The population of western Europe, which had been relatively stagnant for a century and a half, increased by nearly a third in the sixteenth century and stood at about 70 million in 1600.

The increase in population was accompanied by the *enclosure movement,* which had begun in England as early as the thirteenth century. The feudal nobility, in ever-increasing need of cash, fenced off, or enclosed, lands that had formerly been used for communal grazing. Enclosed lands were used to graze sheep to satisfy the booming English wool and textile industries' demand for wool. The sheep brought good prices, and a minimal amount of labor was needed to herd them.

The enclosure movement reached its peak in the late fifteenth and sixteenth centuries when, in some areas, as many as three-fourths to nine-tenths of the tenants were forced out of the countryside and into the cities to try to support themselves. The enclosures and the increasing population further destroyed the remaining feudal ties, creating a large, new labor force—a labor force without land, without any tools or instruments of production, and with only their labor power to sell. This migration to the cities meant more labor for the capitalist industries, more men for the armies and navies, more men to colonize new lands, and more potential consumers, or buyers of products.

Another important source of change was the intellectual awakening of the sixteenth century, which fostered scientific progress that was promptly put to practical use in navigation. The telescope and the compass enabled men to navigate much more accurately for much greater distances. Hence, the "Age of Exploration." Within a short period of time, Europeans had charted sea routes to India, Africa, and the Americas. These discoveries had a twofold importance. First, they resulted in a rapid and large flow of precious metals into Europe, and second, they ushered in a period of colonization.

Between 1300 and 1500, European gold and silver production had stagnated. The rapidly expanding capitalist trade and the extension of the market system into city and countryside had led to an acute shortage of money. Because money consisted primarily of gold and silver coin, the need for these metals was critical. Beginning around 1450, this situation was alleviated somewhat when the Portuguese began extracting metals from the African Gold Coast, but the general shortage continued until the middle of the sixteenth century. After that date, there occurred such a large inflow of gold and silver from the Americas that Europe experienced the most rapid and long-lasting inflation in history.

During the sixteenth century, prices rose in Europe between 150 and 400 percent, depending upon the country or region chosen. Prices of manufactured goods rose much more rapidly than either rents or wages. In fact, the disparity between prices and wages continued until late in the seventeenth century. This meant that the landlord class (or feudal nobility) and the working class both suffered, because their income rose less rapidly than did their expenses. The capitalist class was the great beneficiary of the price revolution. They received larger and larger profits as they paid lower real wages and bought materials that appreciated greatly as they held them as inventories.

These larger profits were accumulated as capital. *Capital* refers to the materials that are necessary for production, trade, and commerce. It consists of all tools, equipment, factories, raw materials and goods in process, means of transporting goods, and money. The essence of the capitalist system is the existence of a class of capitalists who own the capital stock. It is by virtue of their ownership of this capital that they derive their profits. These profits are then plowed back, or used to augment the capital stock. The further accumulation of capital leads to more profits, which leads to more accumulation, and the system continues in an upward spiral.

The name *capitalism* describes this system of profit-seeking and accumulation very well. Capital is the source of profits and hence the source of further accumulation of capital. But this chicken–egg process had to have a beginning. The substantial initial accumulation, or *primitive accumulation,* of capital took place in the period under consideration. The four most important sources of the initial accumulation of capital were (1) the rapidly growing volume of trade and commerce, (2) the putting-out system of industry, (3) the enclosure movement, and (4) the great price inflation. There were several other sources of initial accumulations, some of which were somewhat less respectable and often forgotten, for example, colonial plunder, piracy, and the slave trade.

During the sixteenth and seventeenth centuries, the putting-out system was extended until it was common in most types of manufacturing. Although this was still not the modern type of factory production, the system's increased degree of specialization led to significant increases in productivity. Technical improvements in shipbuilding and navigation also lowered transportation costs. Thus, during this period, capitalist production and trade and commerce thrived and grew very rapidly. The new capitalist class (or middle class or bourgeoisie) slowly but inexorably replaced the nobility as the class that dominated the economic and social system.

The emergence of the new nation-states signaled the beginnings of the transition to a new dominant class. The new monarchs usually drew on the bourgeois capitalist class for support in their efforts to defeat feudal rivals and unify the state under one central power. This unification freed the merchants from the feudal maze of different rules, regulations, laws, weights and measures, and moneys; consolidated many markets; and provided military protection for commercial ventures. In return, the monarch relied on the capitalists for much-needed sources of revenues.

Although England was nominally unified much earlier, it was not until Henry VII (1485–1509) founded the line of Tudor monarchs that England was unified in fact. Henry VIII (1509–1547) and Elizabeth I (1558–1603) were able to complete the work of nation-building only because they had the support of Parliament, which represented the middle classes of the shires and boroughs. In the revolutions of 1648 and 1688, the supremacy of Parliament, or of the bourgeois middle classes, was finally established.

The other important early capitalist nation-states also came into existence in this same period. In France, Louis XI (1461–1483) was the first king to unify France effectively since the time of Charlemagne.

The marriage in 1469 of Ferdinand of Aragon and Isabella of Castile, and their subsequent defeat of the Moors, led to the unification of Spain. The Dutch republic, the fourth of the important early nation-states, did not win its independence until 1690, when they finally expelled their Spanish oppressors.

By the late sixteenth and early seventeenth centuries, most of the large cities in England, France, Spain, and the Low Countries (Belgium and Holland) had been transformed into thriving capitalist economies, dominated by the merchant-capitalists who controlled not only commerce but also much of the manufacturing. In the modern nation-states, coalitions of monarchs and capitalists had wrested effective power from the feudal nobility in many important areas, especially those related to production and commerce. This period of early capitalism is generally referred to as *mercantilism.*

mercantilism: feudal paternalism in early capitalism

The earliest phase of mercantilism, usually called *bullionism,* originated in the period (discussed above) during which Europe was experiencing an acute shortage of gold and silver bullion, and hence there was not enough money to service the rapidly expanding volume of trade. Bullionist policies were designed to attract a flow of gold and silver into a country and to keep them there by prohibiting their export. These restrictions lasted from the late Middle Ages into the sixteenth and seventeenth centuries.

Spain, the country into which most of the gold from the Americas flowed, applied bullionist restrictions over the longest period and imposed the most severe penalty for the export of gold and silver: death! Yet the needs of trade were so pressing and such large profits could be made by importing foreign commodities that even in Spain merchant-capitalists succeeded in bribing corrupt officials or in smuggling large quantities of bullion out of the country. Spanish bullion rapidly found its way all over Europe and was, to a large extent, responsible for the long period of inflation described above. Spain did not legalize the export of gold and silver until long after the bullionist restrictions had been removed in England and Holland in the middle of the sixteenth century.

After the bullionist period, the mercantilists' desire to maximize the gold and silver within a country took the form of attempts by the government to create a favorable balance of trade. A *favorable balance of trade* meant to them that money payments into the country would be greater than money flowing out of the country. Thus exports of goods as well as such things as shipping and insuring, when they were performed by countrymen and paid for by foreigners, were encouraged, and imports of goods and shipping and insurance charges paid to foreigners were discouraged. A favorable balance of trade would ensure the augmentation of the country's treasure. Even though some gold and silver would be paid out in the process, more would come in than would leave.

One of the most important types of policies designed to increase the value of exports and decrease the value of imports was the creation of monopolies of trade. A country such as England could buy most cheaply (from a backward area, for example) if only one English merchant bargained with the foreigners involved, rather than having several competing English merchants bidding the price up in an effort to capture the business. Similarly, English merchants could sell their goods to foreigners for much higher prices if there was only one seller rather than several sellers bidding the price down to attract each other's customers.

The English government could prohibit English merchants from competing in an area where such a monopoly had been established. It was much more difficult, however, to keep out French, Dutch, or Spanish merchants. Various governments attempted to exclude such rival foreign merchants by establishing colonial empires that could be controlled by the mother country to ensure a monopoly of trade. Colonial possessions could thereby furnish cheap raw materials to the mother country and purchase expensive manufactured goods in return.

In addition to the creation of monopolies, all the western European countries (with the exception of Holland) applied extensive regulations to the businesses of exporting and importing. These regulations were probably most comprehensive in England, where exporters who found it difficult to compete with foreigners were given tax refunds or, if that was not enough, they were subsidized. Export duties were placed on a long list of raw materials to keep them within England. Thus, the price English merchant-manufacturers would have to pay for these raw materials would be minimized. Sometimes, when these items were in short supply for British manufacturers, the state would completely prohibit their export. The English textile industry received this type of protection. In the early eighteenth century, it accounted for about one-half of that country's exports. The English prohibited the export of most raw materials and semifinished products such as sheep, wool, yarn, and worsted, which were used by the textile industry.

Measures aimed at discouraging imports were also widespread. The importation of some commodities was prohibited, and other commodities had such high duties that they were nearly eliminated from trade. Special emphasis was placed on protecting England's principal export industries from foreign competitors attempting to cut into the export industries' domestic markets.

Of course, all these restrictions profited some capitalists and harmed others. As would be expected, coalitions of special-interest groups were always working to maintain the restrictions or to extend them into different areas in different ways. Attempts such as the English Navigation Acts of 1651 and 1660 were made to promote the use of British ships (both British-made and British-manned) in both import and export trade. All these types of regulations of foreign trade and shipping were designed to augment the flow of money into the country while decreasing the outflow. Needless to say, many of the measures also stemmed from appeals and pressures by special interests.

In addition to these restrictions on foreign trade, there was a maze of restrictions and regulations aimed at controlling domestic production. Besides the tax exemptions, subsidies, and other privileges used to encourage larger output by industries that were important exporters, the state also engaged in extensive regulation of production methods and of the quality of produced goods. In France, the regime of Louis XIV codified, centralized, and extended the older decentralized guild controls. Specific techniques of production were made mandatory, and extensive quality control measures were enacted, with inspectors appointed in Paris charged with enforcing these laws at the local level. Jean Baptiste Colbert, Louis XIV's famous minister and economic advisor, was responsible for the establishment of extensive and minute regulations. In the textile industry, for example, the width of a piece of cloth and the precise number of threads contained within it were rigidly specified by the government.

In England, the Statute of Artificers (1563) effectively transferred to the state the functions of the old craft guilds. It led to central control of the training of industrial workers, of conditions of employment, and of allocation of the labor force among different types of occupations. The regulation of wages, of the quality of many goods, and of other details of domestic production was also tried in England during this period.

What was the source of this extensive state control of trade, commerce, and domestic production? It might seem at first glance that the state was merely using its powers to promote the special interests of capitalists. This view is reinforced by the fact that most of the important writers of this period who dealt with economic issues were either merchants or employees of merchants. Undoubtedly, many of the particular statutes and regulatory measures were backed by special interests who benefited handsomely from these measures.

However, the rising new middle class of merchant and industrial capitalists were often constrained in their pursuit of profits by the maze of state regulations. Therefore, throughout the period, one finds extensive arguments advanced by these capitalists and their spokesmen for greater freedom from state controls. Economic regulation increasingly became anathema to the capitalists and their spokesmen. In fact, the mercantilist period represents an era in which an outdated economic ideology, the medieval version of the Christian corporate ethic, came into increasingly sharp conflict with a new social and economic order with which it was incompatible. It is this conflict with which Chapter 3 will be concerned.

summary

A series of profound changes resulted in the decline of feudalism and the rise of a new, market-oriented economy. Perhaps the most important of these changes was the improvements in agricultural technology that occurred between the eleventh century and the end of the thirteenth century. These improvements in farming techniques were the original force that set into motion a centuries-long chain of events that ushered in capitalism.

Population grew rapidly and urban concentration increased, which led to a resurgence of long-distance trade. In the cities, the putting-out system was created to produce items that were sold in this trade. This, in turn, led to an urban–rural specialization that could only be accomplished by the monetization of economic tasks and productive activities. The transformation of feudal social relationships into market cash relations destroyed the social base of feudalism. Attempts to preserve the feudal system resulted in bloody suppressions of peasant revolts.

The new capitalist market system was ushered in by the enclosure movement, the intellectual awakening, world exploration, the discovery of large quantities of precious metals, the price inflation of the sixteenth and seventeenth centuries, and the creation of the new nation-states.

In the early stages of capitalism, mercantilist policies resulted in extensive government intervention into market processes, particularly those related to international commerce. These policies were generally aimed at securing high profits for the great merchant trading companies, raising revenues for national governments, and more generally, bringing a maximum of precious metal into the country concerned.

chapter 3
the conflict in mercantilist thought

The Christian corporate ethic, with its condemnation of acquisitive behavior, conflicted with the interests of merchants throughout the feudal period. As the importance of trade and commerce grew, the intensity of the conflict grew. There were two principal themes underlying the development of English mercantilism.[1] "One was the biblical injunction to promote the general welfare and common good of God's corporate world and its creatures. The second was the growing propensity to define God's estate as the civil society in which the Christian resided."[2] During this period, the state began to take over the role of the church in interpreting and enforcing the Christian corporate ethic. The basic issue for the earliest formulators of mercantilist policies was whether the growing merchant class was to be allowed to pursue its profits recklessly, regardless of the social and economic consequences of that pursuit. The Christian ethic demanded that the activities of the merchants be checked and controlled in the interest of the welfare of the entire community.

1 We will concentrate primarily on English mercantilism in this chapter because industrial capitalism developed first in England and because most of the ideas in the capitalist ideology that we will discuss in Chapter 4 were developed in England.

2 William Appleman Williams, *The Countours of American History* (Chicago: Quadrangle Books, 1966), p. 33.

the medieval origins of mercantilist policies

The first indications of a mercantilistic type of economic policy can be traced to Edward I (1272–1307), who evicted several foreign economic enterprises from England, established the English wool trade in Antwerp, and made various attempts to control commerce within England. A short time later, Edward III significantly extended these policies of economic control. The long war with France (1333–1360) led him to attempt to mitigate the harsh effects that the wartime inflation was having on the laborers. He did this by fixing wages and prices in a ratio that was more favorable to the laborers. In return for this aid, Edward required all men to work at whatever jobs were available. "As this *quid pro quo* indicates, mercantilism was grounded in the idea of a mutual, corporate responsibility. God's way was based on such reciprocal respect and obligation, and Jerusalem provided the example to be followed."[3]

Richard II (1377–1399) extended and systematized his predecessors' policies. The principal problems facing England during his reign were the social and economic conflict that led to the Peasant's Rebellion of 1381 (see Chapter 2) and the necessity of countering foreign competition more effectively. The latter problem led to the Navigation Act of 1381, which was designed to favor English shippers and traders and to bring gold and silver into England. This money was needed for his program of building England into a "well and rightly governed kingdom" in which greater economic security for all would mitigate the social tensions that existed.

Henry VII (1485–1509) renewed these policies. He commissioned numerous voyages of explorers and adventurers and attempted in various ways to secure legislation and negotiate treaties advantageous to English merchants. At the same time, he subjected merchants to many controls and regulations imposed by the crown, for he believed that the unlimited pursuit of self-interest in the quest for profits was often harmful to general social interests and harmony.

Henry was still balancing feudal and capitalist interests; neither was dominant enough to persuade him to favor one over the other. The rapid growth of mining and wool-raising during his reign led to an unfortunate neglecting of food production. Moreover, the general excesses of the merchants had alienated both the peasants and the

[3] Williams, op. cit., p. 34. The following several pages draw heavily on Williams' excellent book.

agrarian aristocracy. The merchants seemed to understand these problems and accepted a relationship in which, in return for crown policies that would benefit them in foreign dealings, they submitted to domestic regulation of manufacturing and commerce.

the secularization of church functions

During the reign of Henry VIII, England broke with Roman Catholicism. This event was significant because it marked the final secularization (in England at least) of the functions of the medieval church. Under Henry, "the state in the form of God's monarchy assumed the role and the functions of the old universal church. What Henry had done in his own blunt way was to sanctify the processes of this world."[4] During his reign as well as during those of Elizabeth I, James I, and Charles I (1558–1649) there was widespread social unrest. The cause of this unrest was poverty, and the cause of much of the poverty was unemployment.

The enclosure movements (discussed in Chapter 2) were responsible for much of the unemployment. Another factor, however, was the decline in the export of woolens in the last half of the sixteenth century, which created a great deal of unemployment in England's most important manufacturing industry. There were also frequent commercial crises similar to, but without the regularity of, the depression phase of later business cycles. In addition to these factors, seasonal unemployment put many workers out of work for as many as four months of the year.

The people could no longer look to the Catholic church for relief from widespread unemployment and poverty. Destruction of the power of the church had eliminated the organized system of charity. The state attempted to assume responsibility for the general welfare of society. In order to do this, "England's leaders undertook a general, coordinated program to reorganize and rationalize . . . industry by establishing specifications of standards of production and marketing."[5] All these measures were designed to stimulate English trade and alleviate the unemployment problem.

In fact, it appears that the desire to achieve full employment is the unifying theme of most policy measures advocated by mercantilist writers. The mercantilists preferred measures designed to stimulate foreign rather than domestic trade "because they believed it contributed more to employment, to the nation's wealth and to

4 Ibid., p. 36.

5 Ibid., p. 40.

national power. The writers after 1600 stressed the inflationary effect of an excess of exports over imports and the consequent increase in employment which inflation produced."[6]

Among the other measures taken to encourage industry during this period was the issuance of patents of monopoly. The first important patent was granted in 1561, during the reign of Elizabeth I. Monopoly rights were given in order to encourage inventions and to establish new industries. These rights were severely abused, as might be expected. Moreover, they led to a complex system of special privileges and patronage and a host of other evils, which outraged most mercantilist writers every bit as much as similar abuses outraged late nineteenth-century American reformers. The evils of monopoly led to the Statute of Monopolies of 1624, which outlawed all monopolies except those that involved genuine inventions or that would be instrumental in promoting a favorable balance of payments. Of course, these loopholes were large, and abuses continued almost unchecked.

The Statute of Artificers (1563) specified conditions of employment and length of apprenticeships, provided for periodic wage assessments, and established maximum rates that could be paid to laborers. The statute is important because it illustrates the fact that the crown's paternalistic ethic never led to any attempt to elevate the status of the laboring classes. Monarchs of this period felt obliged to protect the working classes but, like their predecessors in the Middle Ages, believed that the working classes should be kept in their proper place. Maximum wage rates were designed to protect the capitalists, and furthermore, the justices who set these maximums and who enforced the statute generally belonged to the employing class themselves. It is probable that these maximums reduced the real wages of laborers because prices generally rose faster than wages during the succeeding years.

Poor laws passed in 1531 and 1536 attempted to deal with the problems of unemployment, poverty, and misery then widespread in England. The first sought to distinguish between "deserving" and "undeserving" poor: Only the deserving poor were allowed to beg. The second decreed that each individual parish throughout England was responsible for its poor and that the parish should, through voluntary contributions, maintain a poor fund. This proved to be completely inadequate, and the "pauper problem" grew increasingly severe.

Finally, in 1572, the state accepted the principle that the poor would have to be supported by tax funds and enacted a compulsory "poor rate." And in 1576, "houses of correction" for "incorrigible vagrants"

[6] William D. Grampp, *Economic Liberalism*, vol. 1 (New York: Random House, 1965), p. 59.

were authorized and provisions were made for the parish to purchase raw materials to be worked up by the more tractable paupers and vagrants. Between that time and the close of the sixteenth century, several other poor law statutes were passed.

The Poor Law of 1601 was the Tudor attempt to integrate all these into one consistent framework. Its main provisions included the formal recognition of the right of the poor to receive relief, the imposition of compulsory poor rates at the parish level, and the provision for differential treatment for various classes of the poor. The aged and the sick could receive help in their homes; pauper children who were too young to be apprenticed in a trade were to be boarded out; the deserving poor and unemployed were to be given work as provided for in the act of 1576; and incorrigible vagrants were to be sent to houses of correction and prisons.[7]

From the foregoing discussion, it is possible to conclude that the period of English mercantilism that preceded the English civil war was characterized by an acceptance, in the spirit of the Christian corporate ethic, of the idea that "the state had an obligation to serve society by accepting and discharging the responsibility for the general welfare."[8] The various statutes passed during this period "were predicated upon the idea that poverty, instead of being a personal sin was a function of the economic system."[9] They acknowledged that those who were the victims of the deficiencies of the economic system should be cared for by those who benefited from the system.

the rise of individualism

After the Glorious Revolution of 1688, the English government was dominated by the gentry and the middle-class capitalists. The medieval world view that underlay the Christian corporate ethic was eclipsed. A fundamental shift in the philosophy of the role of the state in society took place over the next 100 years. In 1776, with the publication of Adam Smith's *The Wealth of Nations,* a new individualistic philosophy—classical liberalism[10]—had definitely gained the ascendancy in England. This individualistic philosophy

[7] For an extension of this discussion of the poor laws, see Arthur Birnie, *An Economic History of the British Isles* (London: Methuen, 1936), chaps. 12 and 18.

[8] Williams, op. cit., p. 41.

[9] Ibid., p. 44.

[10] We use the adjective *classical* to differentiate the traditional liberal world view from what is called liberalism in the twentieth century. This distinction is further clarified in Chapter 4.

had existed throughout the mercantilist period, struggling to break the hold of the older corporate world view. In the end, the new classical liberalism prevailed because it, not the older, essentially medieval world view, reflected the needs of the new capitalist order.

In condemning greed, acquisitive behavior, and the desire to accumulate wealth, the medieval Christian corporate ethic condemned what had become the capitalist order's dominant motive force. The capitalist market economy, which had been extended by the late eighteenth century to almost every phase of production, demanded self-seeking, acquisitive behavior for its successful functioning. In this context new theories about human behavior began to emerge. Writers began to assert that selfish, egoistic motives were the primary if not the only motives that moved men to action.

This interpretation of man's behavior is expressed in the writings of many important thinkers of the period. Many philosophers and social theorists began to assert that every human act was related to self-preservation and hence was egoistic in the most fundamental sense. The English nobleman Sir Robert Filmer was greatly alarmed by the large number of people who spoke of "the natural freedom of mankind, a new, plausible and dangerous opinion" with anarchistic implications.[11] Thomas Hobbes' *Leviathan,* published in 1651, trenchantly articulated a widely held opinion—that all human motives stem from a desire for whatever promotes the "vital motion" of the organism (man). Hobbes believed that all men were, by nature, self-seeking and egoistic, and that all man's motives, even compassion, were merely so many disguised species of self-interest: "Grief for the calamity of another is *pity,* and ariseth from the imagination that the like calamity may befall himself; and therefore is called . . . *compassion,* and . . . fellow-feeling. . . ."[12]

Except for the few special interests that benefited from the extensive restrictions and regulations of commerce and manufacturing during this period, most capitalists felt constrained and inhibited by state regulations in their quest for profits. The individualistic and egoistic doctrines were eagerly embraced by such men. This view began to dominate economic thinking, even among the mercantilists. One careful history asserts: "most of the mercantilist . . . policy assumed that self-interest governs individual conduct. . . ."[13]

The majority of mercantilist writers were either capitalists or employees of the great capitalist trading companies. It was quite

11 Lee Cameron McDonald, *Western Political Theory: The Modern Age* (New York: Harcourt Brace Jovanovich, 1962), p. 29.

12 Quoted in Harry K. Giretz, *The Evolution of Liberalism* (New York: Colliers, 1963), pp. 28–29.

13 Grampp, op. cit., p. 69.

natural for them to perceive the motives of the capitalists as universal. From the capitalists' views of the nature of man and from their needs to be free of the extensive economic restrictions that inhibited them in the conduct of their everyday business grew the philosophy of individualism that provided the basis of classical liberalism. Against the well-ordered, paternalistic view that Europe had inherited from the feudal society, they asserted "the view that the human person ought to be independent, self-directing, autonomous, free—ought to be, that is, an individual, a unit distinguished from the social mass rather than submerged in it."[14]

protestantism and the individualistic ethic

One of the most important examples of this individualistic and middle-class philosophy was the Protestant theology that emerged from the Reformation. The new middle-class capitalists wanted to be free not only of economic restrictions that encumbered manufacturing and commerce but also of the moral opprobrium that the Catholic church had heaped upon their motives and activities. Protestantism not only freed them from religious condemnation but eventually made virtues of the selfish, egoistic, and acquisitive motives the medieval church had so despised![15]

The principal originators of the Protestant movement were quite close to the Catholic position on such questions as usury and the just price. On most social issues they were deeply conservative. During the German peasant revolt of 1524, Luther wrote a virulent pamphlet, *Against the Murdering Hordes of Peasants,* in which he said princes should "knock down, strangle and stab. . . . Such wonderful times are these that a prince can merit heaven better with bloodshed than another with prayer." His advice contributed to the general atmosphere in which the slaughter of over 100,000 peasants was carried out with an air of religious righteousness.

Yet despite the conservatism of the founders of Protestantism, this religious outlook contributed to the growing influence of the new individualistic philosophy. The basic tenet of Protestantism, which laid the groundwork for religious attitudes that were to sanction middle-class business practices, was the doctrine that men were justified by faith rather than by works. The Catholic church had

[14] McDonald, op. cit., p. 16.

[15] The classic studies of the relationship between Protestantism and capitalism are Max Weber, *The Protestant Ethic and the Spirit of Capitalism* (New York: Scribner's, 1958), and Richard H. Tawney, *Religion and the Rise of Capitalism* (New York: Mentor Books, 1954).

taught that men were justified by *works,* which generally meant by ceremonies and rituals. In the Catholic view, no man could be justified on his own merit alone. "Justification by works . . . did not mean that an individual could save himself: it meant that he could be saved through the Church. Hence the power of the clergy. Compulsory confession, the imposition of penance on the whole population . . . together with the possibility of withholding absolution, gave the priests a terrifying power."[16] These powers also created a situation in which the medieval doctrines of the Catholic church were not easily abandoned and in which the individual was still subordinated to society (as represented by the church).

The Protestant doctrine of justification by faith asserted that *motives* were more important than specific acts or rituals. Faith was "nothing else but the truth of the heart."[17] Each man had to search his own heart to discover if his acts stemmed from a pure heart and faith in God. Each man had to judge for himself. This individualistic reliance on each person's private conscience appealed strongly to the new middle-class artisans and small merchants. "When the business man of sixteenth and seventeenth century Geneva, Amsterdam or London looked into his inmost heart, he found that God had planted there a deep respect for the principle of private property. . . . Such men felt quite genuinely and strongly that their economic practices, though they might conflict with the traditional law of the old church, were not offensive to God. On the contrary: they glorified God."[18]

It was through this insistence on the individual's own interpretation of God's will that the "Puritans tried to spiritualize [the new] economic processes" and eventually came to believe that "God instituted the market and exchange."[19] However, it was only a matter of time before the Protestants expounded dogma that they expected everyone to accept. But the new dogma was radically different from medieval doctrines. The new doctrines stressed the necessity of doing well at one's earthly calling as the best way to please God and emphasized diligence and hard work.

The older Christian distrust of riches was "translated" into a condemnation of extravagance and needless dissipation of wealth. Thus, the Protestant ethic stressed the importance of asceticism and abstemious frugality. A theologian, who has studied the connection between religion and capitalism, summed up the relationship in this way: "The religious value set upon constant, systematic, efficient

[16] Christopher Hill, "Protestantism and the Rise of Capitalism," in D. S. Landes, ed., *The Rise of Capitalism* (New York: Macmillan, 1966), p. 43.

[17] Ibid.

[18] Ibid., pp. 46–47.

[19] Ibid., p. 49.

work in one's calling as the readiest means of securing the certainty of salvation and of glorifying God became a most powerful agency in economic expansion. The rigid limitations of consumption on the one hand and the methodical intensification of production on the other could have but one result—the accumulation of capital."[20] Thus, although neither Calvin nor Luther was a spokesman for the new middle-class capitalist, within the context of the new religious individualism the capitalists found a religion in which, over time, "profits . . . [came to be] looked upon as willed by God, as a mark of his favor and a proof of success in one's calling."[21]

the economic policies of individualism

Throughout the mercantilist period, this new individualism led to innumerable protests against the subordination of economic affairs to the will of the state. From the middle of the seventeenth century, almost all mercantilist writers condemned state-granted monopolies and other forms of protection and favoritism in the internal economy (as opposed to international commerce). Many believed that in a competitive market that pitted buyer against buyer, seller against seller, and buyer against seller, society would benefit most greatly if the price were left free to fluctuate and find its proper (market equilibrating) level. One of the earliest mercantilist writers of importance, John Hales, argued that agricultural productivity could best be improved if the husbandmen were allowed to

> have more profit by it than they have, and liberty to sell it at all times, and to all places, as freely as men may do their other things. But then no doubt, the price of corn would rise, specially at the first more than at length; yet that price would provoke every man to set plough in the ground, to husband waste grounds, yes to turn the lands which be enclosed from pasture to arable land; for every man will gladder follow that wherein they see the more profit and gains, and thereby must need ensue both plenty of corn, and also much treasure should be brought into this realm by occasion thereof; and besides that plenty of other victuals increased among us.[22]

This belief—that restrictions on production and trade within a nation were harmful to the interests of everyone concerned—became

[20] Kemper Fullerton, "Calvinism and Capitalism; an Explanation of the Weber Thesis," in Robert W. Green, ed., *Protestantism and Capitalism: The Weber Thesis and Its Critics* (Lexington, Mass.: Heath, 1959), p. 19.

[21] Ibid., p. 18.

[22] Quoted in Grampp, op. cit., p. 78.

increasingly widespread in the late seventeenth and early eighteenth centuries. Numerous statements of this view can be found in the works of such writers as Malynes, Petty, North, Law, and Child.[23] Of these men, perhaps Sir Dudley North (1641–1691) was the earliest clear spokesman for the individualistic ethic that was to become the basis for classical liberalism. North believed that all men were motivated primarily by self-interest and that they should be left alone to compete in a free market if the public welfare were to be maximized. He argued that whenever merchants or capitalists advocated special laws to regulate production or commerce, "they usually esteem the immediate Interest of their own to be the common Measure of Good and Evil. And there are many, who to gain a little in their own Trades, care not how much others suffer; and each man strives that all others may be forced in their dealings to act subserviently for his Profit, but under the cover of the Publick."[24] The public welfare would best be served, North believed, if most of the restrictive laws that bestowed special privileges were entirely removed.

In 1714, Bernard Mandeville published *The Fable of the Bees: or Private Vices, Publick Benefits,* in which he put forth the seemingly strange paradox that the vices most despised in the older moral code, if practiced by all, would result in the greatest public good. Selfishness, greed, and acquisitive behavior, he maintained, all tended to contribute to industriousness and a thriving economy. The answer to the paradox was, of course, that what had been vices in the eyes of the medieval moralists were the very motive forces that propelled the new capitalist system. And in the view of the new religious, moral, and economic philosophies of the capitalist period, these motives were no longer vices.

The capitalists had struggled throughout the mercantilist period to free themselves from all restrictions in their quest for profits. These restrictions had resulted from the paternalistic laws that were the remnants of the feudal version of the Christian corporate ethic. The paternalistic Christian ethic was simply not compatible with the new economic system that functioned on the basis of strict contractual obligations between persons rather than on that of traditional personal ties. Merchants and capitalists who invested large sums in market ventures could not depend on the forces of custom to protect their investment.

Profit-seeking could only be effective in a society based on the protection of property rights and the enforcement of impersonal contractual commitments between individuals. The new ideology that

23 Ibid., pp. 77–81.

24 Quoted in Robert Lekackmen, ed., *The Varieties of Economics,* vol. I (New York: Meridian, 1962), p. 185.

was firmly taking root in the late seventeenth and eighteenth centuries justified these motives and relations between individuals. It is to a consideration of this new individualistic philosophy of classical liberalism that we turn in Chapter 4.

summary

There is a basic continuity between medieval and mercantilist social thought. State intervention into economic processes was originally justified in terms of the medieval Christian notion that those to whom God had given power were obligated to use this power to promote the general welfare and common good of all society. In early capitalism, the state began to assume many of the roles that the church had formerly held.

The Christian corporate ethic, however, had thoroughly condemned the acquisitive behavior that was to become the dominant motive force of the new capitalist system. It was, therefore, necessary to create a new philosophical and ideological point of view that morally justified individualization, greed, and profit-seeking.

Protestantism and the new philosophies of individualism furnished the bases for this new ideology. The economic writings of the mercantilists reflected this new individualism. The new point of view emphasized the need for greater freedom for capitalists to seek profits, and hence the need for less government intervention in the market. Thus, the presence of two fundamentally different general points of view in mercantilist writings created an intellectual conflict that was not resolved until the classical liberal philosophy, including classical economics, effectively ferreted out all remnants of the medieval Christian corporate ethic. In Chapter 4, we shall examine the industrial revolution and the ascendance of the classical liberal ideology of capitalism.

chapter 4
classical liberalism and the triumph of industrial capitalism

A single theme runs through the works of the mercantilist writers (considered in the latter part of Chapter 3) that distinguishes them from the later classical liberal writers. They argued for a minimum of internal restriction and regulation, *but* they favored an active governmental policy designed to further England's commerce in the international trading markets. The classical liberals, however, advocated free trade internationally as well as domestically. In this chapter, we examine the changes in England's commercial position that encouraged her economists to favor free trade.

the industrial revolution

Between 1700 and 1770, the foreign markets for English goods grew much faster than her domestic markets. During the period 1700–1750, output in domestic industries increased by 7 percent, while that in export industries increased by 76 percent. For the period 1750–1770, the figures are 7 percent and 80 percent. This rapidly increasing foreign demand for English manufactures was the single most important cause of the most fundamental transformation of human life in history: the industrial revolution.

Eighteenth-century England was an economy with a well-developed market and one in which the traditional anticapitalist market bias in attitudes and ideology had been greatly weakened. In this England, larger outputs of manufactured goods produced at lower prices meant ever-increasing profits. Thus, profit seeking was the motive that, stimulated by increasing foreign demand, accounts for the virtual explosion of technological innovations that occurred in the late eighteenth and early nineteenth centuries—and radically transformed all England and eventually most of the world.

The textile industry was the most important in the early industrial revolution. In 1700, the woolen industry had persuaded the government to ban the import of Indian-made "calicoes" (cotton), and thus had secured a protected home market for domestic producers. As outlined above, rising foreign demand spurred mechanization of the industry.

More specifically, an imbalance between the spinning and weaving processes led to many of the innovations. The spinning wheel was not as productive as the hand loom, especially after the 1730s, when the flying shuttle was invented and the weaving process was speeded up considerably. This imbalance led to three inventions that reversed it: the spinning jenny, developed in the 1760s, with which one person could spin several threads simultaneously; the water frame, invented in 1768, which improved spinning by using both rollers and spindles in the process; and the mule, developed in the 1780s, which combined features of the other two and permitted the application of steam power. These new inventions could be used most economically in factories near the source of the water power (and later steam power). Richard Arkwright, who claimed to be the inventor of the water frame, raised sufficient capital to put a great many factories into operation, each employing anywhere from 150 to 600 persons. Others followed his example, and textile manufacturing in England was rapidly transformed from a cottage to a factory industry.

The iron industry was also very important in the early drive to mechanized factory production. In the early eighteenth century, England's iron industry was quite inconsequential. Charcoal was still used for smelting, as had been done since prehistoric times. By this time, however, the forests surrounding the iron mines were almost completely depleted. England was forced to import pig iron from her colonies, as well as from Sweden, Germany, and Spain. In 1709, Abraham Darby developed a process for making coke from coal for use in the smelting process.

Despite the relative abundance of coal near the iron mines, it was not until the latter part of the eighteenth century (when the military demands on the arms and munitions industries were very great) that the iron industry began using coke extensively. This increased demand led to the development of the puddling process, which eliminated the excess carbon left by the coke. A whole series of innovations followed, including the rolling mill, the blast furnace, the steam hammer, and metal-turning lathes. All these inventions led to a very rapid expansion of the iron and coal-mining industries, which permitted the increasingly widespread use of machines made of iron in a great variety of industries.

Entrepreneurs in many other industries saw the possibilities for larger profits if they could increase output and lower costs. In this period, there was a "veritable outburst of inventive activity":

> During the second half of the eighteenth century, interest in technical innovations became unusually intensive. For a hundred years prior to 1760, the number of patents issued during each decade had reached 102 only once, and had otherwise fluctuated between a low of 22 (1700–1709) and a high of 92 (1750–1759). During the following thirty-year period (1760–1789), the average number of patents issued increased from 205 in the 1760's to 294 in the 1770's and 477 in the 1780's.[1]

Undoubtedly the most important of these innovations was the development of the steam engine. Industrial steam engines had been introduced in the early 1700s, but mechanical difficulties had limited their use to the pumping of water in mines. In 1769, James Watt designed an engine with such accurate specifications that the straight thrust of a piston could be translated into rotary motion. A Birmingham manufacturer named Boulton formed a partnership with Watt, and with Boulton's financial resources they were able to go into large-scale production of steam engines. By the turn of the century, steam was rapidly replacing water as the chief source of power in manufacturing. The development of steam power led to profound economic and social changes.

> With this new great event, the invention of the steam engine, the final and most decisive stage of the industrial revolution opened. By liberating it from its last shackles, steam enabled the immense and rapid development of large-scale industry to take place. For the use of steam was not, like that of water, dependent on geographical position and local resources. Whenever coal could be bought at a reasonable price a steam engine could be erected. England had plenty of coal, and by the end of the eighteenth century it was already applied to many different uses, while a network of waterways, made on purpose, enabled it to be carried everywhere very cheaply: the whole country became a privileged land, suitable above all others for

[1] Reinhard Bendix, *Work and Authority in Industry* (New York: Harper & Row, Torchbooks, 1963), p. 27.

> the growth of industry. Factories were now no longer bound to the valleys, where they had grown up in solitude by the side of rapid-flowing streams. It became possible to bring them nearer the markets where their raw materials were bought and their finished products sold, and nearer the centers of population where their labor was recruited. They sprang up near one another and thus, huddled together, gave rise to those huge black industrial cities which the steam engine surrounded with a perpetual cloud of smoke.[2]

The growth in the major manufacturing cities was truly spectacular. For example, the population of Manchester rose from 17,000 in 1760 to 237,000 in 1831 and to 400,000 in 1851. Output of manufactured goods approximately doubled in the last half of the eighteenth century and grew even more rapidly in the early nineteenth century. By 1801, nearly 30 percent of the English work force was employed in manufacturing and mining; by 1831, this figure had risen to over 40 percent. Thus, the industrial revolution transformed England into a country of large urban manufacturing centers, where the factory system was dominant. The result was a very rapid growth of productivity that vaulted England into the position of the greatest economic and political power of the nineteenth century. The effects of the industrial revolution on the lives of the English people will be discussed in Chapter 5.

the rise of classical liberalism

It was during this period of industrialization that the individualistic world view of classical liberalism became the dominant ideology of capitalism.[3] Many of the ideas of classical liberalism had taken root and even gained wide acceptance in the mercantilist period, but it was in the late eighteenth and nineteenth centuries that classical liberalism most completely dominated social, political, and economic thought in England. The Christian corporate ethic was still advanced in the writings of many of the nobility and their allies as well as many socialists, but in this era these expressions were, by and large, dissident minority views.

[2] Paul Mantoux, *The Industrial Revolution in the Eighteenth Century* (New York: Harcourt Brace Jovanovich, 1927), pp. 344–345.

[3] This account of classical liberalism relies heavily on Harry K. Girvetz, *The Evolution of Liberalism* (New York: Collier, 1963), pp. 1–149.

the psychological creed

Classical liberalism's psychological creed was based upon four assumptions about human nature. People were believed to be egoistic, intellectualistic, essentially inert, and atomistic. (See Chapter 3 for a discussion of the egoistic theory of human nature.) The egoism argued by Hobbes furnished the basis for this view, and, in the works of later liberals, especially Jeremy Bentham, it was blended with psychological hedonism: the view that all actions are motivated by the desire to achieve pleasure and avoid pain.

"Nature," Bentham wrote, "has placed mankind under the governance of two sovereign masters, *pain,* and *pleasure.* . . . They govern us in all we do, in all we say, in all we think."[4] Pleasures differed in intensity, Bentham believed, but there were no qualitative differences. He argued that "quantity of pleasure being equal, pushpin is as good as poetry." This theory of human motivation as selfish is found in the writings of many of the most eminent thinkers of the period, including John Locke, Bernard Mandeville, David Hartley, Abraham Tucker, and Adam Smith. Smith's ideas will be examined in some detail later in this chapter.

Man's intellect played a significant role in the classical liberal's scheme of things. Although all motives stemmed from pleasure and pain, the decisions people made about what pleasures or pains to seek or avoid were based on a cool, dispassionate, and rational assessment of the situation. Reason would dictate that all alternatives in a situation be weighed in order to choose that which would maximize pleasure or minimize pain. It is this emphasis on the importance of rational calculation of pleasures and pains (with a corresponding deemphasis of caprice, instinct, habit, custom, or convention) that forms the intellectualistic side of the classical liberal's theory of psychology.

The view that individuals were essentially inert stemmed from the notion that pleasure or the avoidance of pain were men's only motives. If men could see no activities leading to pleasurable conclusions or feared no pain, then they would be inert, motionless, or in simpler terms, just plain lazy. Any kind of exertion or work was viewed as painful and therefore would not be undertaken without the promise of greater pleasure or the avoidance of greater pain. "Aversion," wrote Bentham, "is the emotion—the only emotion—

[4] Jeremy Bentham, "An Introduction to the Principles of Morals and Legislation," In A. I. Melden, ed., *Ethical Theories* (Englewood Cliffs, N.J.: Prentice-Hall, 1955), p. 341.

which labor, taken by itself, is qualified to produce: of any such emotion as *love* or *desire, ease,* which is the *negative* or *absence* of *labor*—ease, not labor—is the object."[5]

The practical outcome of this doctrine (or perhaps the reason for it) was the widespread belief of the time that laborers were incurably lazy. Thus, only a large reward or the fear of starvation and deprivation could force them to work. The Reverend Joseph Townsend put this view very succinctly: "Hunger is not only peaceable, silent and unremitted pressure, but, as the most natural motive to industry and labor, it calls forth the most powerful exertions." Townsend believed that "only the experience of hunger would goad them [laborers] to labor."[6]

This view differed radically from the older, paternalistic ethic which had led to the passage of the Elizabethan Poor Relief Act of 1601. The paternalistic concern for the poor had lasted for two centuries and had culminated in 1795 in the *Speenhamland system,* which guaranteed everyone, able-bodied or not, working or not, a minimal subsistence to be paid by public taxes. It was against this system that the classical liberals railed. They eventually succeeded in passing the Poor Law of 1834, the object of which, according to Dicey, "was in reality to save the property of hard-working men from destruction by putting an end to the monstrous system under which laggards who would not toil for their support lived at the expense of their industrious neighbors. . . ."[7]

Classical liberals were persuaded, however, that the "higher ranks" of men were motivated by ambition. This differentiation of men into different ranks betrayed an implicit elitism in their individualistic doctrines. In order to assure ample effort on the part of the "elite," the classical liberals believed that the state should put the highest priority on the protection of private property. Although the argument began "as an argument for guaranteeing to the worker the fruits of his toil, it has become one of the chief apologies for the institution of private property in general."[8]

The last of the four tenets was atomism which held that the individual was a more fundamental reality than the group or society. "Priority . . . [was] . . . assigned to the ultimate components out of which an aggregate or whole . . . [was] . . . composed; they constituted the fundamental reality."[9] With this notion, the classical liberals rejected the concept, implicit in the Christian corporate

5 Quoted in Girvetz, op. cit., p. 38.

6 Bendix, op. clt., p. 74.

7 Albert V. Dicey, *Law and Public Opinion in England* (2d. ed.; London: Macmillan, 1926), p. 203.

8 Girvetz, op. cit., p. 50.

9 Ibid., p. 41.

ethic, that society was like a family and that the whole and the relationships that made up the whole were more important than any individual. The liberal's individualistic beliefs were inconsistent with the personal and human ties envisioned in the Christian corporate ethic. The group was, for them, no more than the additive total of the individuals that constituted it. They believed that restrictions placed upon the individual by society were generally evil and should be tolerated only when an even worse evil would result without them.

This atomistic psychology can be contrasted to a more socially oriented psychology that would lead to the conclusion that most of the characteristics, habits, ways of perceiving and thinking about the life processes, and the individual's general personality patterns are significantly influenced, if not determined, by the social institutions and social relationships of which he is a part. Atomistic psychology, however, sees the makeup of the individual as somehow independently given. It therefore regards social institutions as both tools for and the handiwork of these individuals. In this view, society exists only because it is useful, and if it were not for this usefulness, each individual could go his own way, discarding society much as he would discard a tool that no longer served its purpose.

the economic creed

Several explanations are necessary for an understanding of why the classical liberals thought society to be so useful. For example, they talked about the "natural gregariousness of men," the need for collective security, and the economic benefits of the division of labor, which society makes possible. The latter was the foundation of the economic creed of classical liberalism, and the creed was crucial to classical liberalism because this philosophy contained what appear to be two contradictory or conflicting assumptions.

On the one hand, the assumption of man's innate egoism had led Hobbes to assert that in the absence of restraints, men's selfish motives would lead to a "natural state" of war, with each man pitted against all others. In this state of nature, Hobbes believed that the life of man was "solitary, poor, nasty, brutish, and short." The only escape from brutal combat was the establishment of some source of absolute power—a central government—to which each man submitted in return for protection from all other men.[10]

On the other hand, one of the cardinal tenets of classical liberalism was that men (or more particularly businessmen) should be free to

[10] Hobbes, "Leviathan," reprinted in Melden, op. cit., pp. 192–205.

give vent to their egoistic drives with a minimum of control or restraint imposed by society. This apparent contradiction was bridged by the liberal economic creed which asserted that if the competitiveness and rivalry of unrestrained egoism existed in a capitalist market setting, then this competition would benefit the individuals involved and all society as well. This view was put forth in the most profound single intellectual achievement of classical liberalism: Adam Smith's *The Wealth of Nations,* published in 1776.

Smith believed that "every individual . . . [was] continually exerting himself to find out the most advantageous employment for whatever capital he can command."[11] Those without capital were always searching for that employment at which the monetary return for their labor would be maximized. If both capitalists and laborers were left alone, self-interest would guide them to use their capital and labor where they were most productive. The search for profits would ensure that what was produced would be what people wanted most and were willing to pay for. Thus, Smith and classical liberals in general were opposed to having some authority or law determine what should be produced. "It is not from the benevolence of the butcher, the brewer, or the baker, that we expect our dinner, but from their regard to their own interest,"[12] wrote Smith. Producers of various goods must compete in the market for the dollars of consumers. That producer who offered a better-quality product would attract more consumers. He therefore would be led by his self-interest to constant improvement of the quality of his product. The producer could also increase profits by cutting his costs of production to a minimum.

Thus, a *free market,* in which producers competed for consumers' dollars in an egoistic quest for more profits, would guarantee the direction of capital and labor to their most productive uses and would ensure the production of the goods consumers wanted and needed most (as measured by their ability and willingness to pay for them). Moreover, the market would lead to a constant striving to improve the quality of products and to organize production in the most efficient and least-costly manner possible. All these beneficial actions would stem directly from the competition of egoistical men, each pursuing his self-interest.

What a far cry from the "solitary, poor, nasty and brutish" world Hobbes thought would result from man's competitiveness. The wonderful social institution that could make all this possible was the free and unrestrained market, the forces of supply and demand. The market, Smith believed, would act as an "invisible hand"

11 Adam Smith, *The Wealth of Nations* (New York: Modern Library, 1937), p. 421.

12 Ibid., p. 14.

channeling selfish, egoistic motives into mutually consistent and complementary activities that would best promote the welfare of all society. And the greatest beauty of it was the complete lack of any need for paternalistic guidance, direction, or restrictions. Freedom from coercion in a capitalist market economy was compatible with a natural orderliness in which the welfare of each, as well as the welfare of all society (which was, after all, only the aggregate of the individuals that constitute it), would be maximized. In Smith's words, each producer

> intends only his own security; and by directing that industry in such a manner as its produce may be of the greatest value, he intends only his own gain, and he is in this, as in many other cases, led by an invisible hand to promote an end which was no part of his intention. Nor is it always the worse for the society that it was not part of it. By pursuing his own interest he frequently promotes that of society more effectually than when he really intends to promote it. I have never known much good done by those who affected to trade for the public good. It is an affectation, indeed, not very common among merchants, and very few words need be employed in dissuading them from it.[13]

With this statement it is evident that Smith had a philosophy totally antithetical to the paternalism of the Christian corporate ethic. The Christian notion of the rich promoting the security and well-being of the poor through paternalistic control and almsgiving contrasts sharply with Smith's picture of a capitalist who is concerned only with "his own advantage, indeed, and not that of the society. . . . But the study of his own advantage naturally, or rather necessarily leads him to prefer that employment which is most advantageous to the society."[14]

Not only would the free and unfettered market channel productive energies and resources into their most valuable uses, but it would also lead to continual economic progress. Economic well-being depended upon the capacity of an economy to produce. Productive capacity in turn depended upon the accumulation of capital and the division of labor. When one man produced everything he needed for himself and his family, production was very inefficient. But if men subdivided tasks, each producing only that commodity for which his own abilities best suited him, productivity increased. For such a subdivision of tasks, a market was necessary in order to exchange goods. In the market, each person could get all the items he needed but did not produce.

[13] Ibid., p. 423.

[14] Ibid., p. 421.

This increase in productivity could be extended further if the production of each commodity were broken down into many steps or stages. Each person would then work on only one stage of the production of one commodity. In order to achieve a division of labor of this degree, it was necessary to have many specialized tools and other equipment. It was also necessary that all the stages of production for a particular commodity be brought together and coordinated as, for example, in a factory. Thus, an increasingly fine division of labor required the accumulation of capital in the form of tools, equipment, factories, and money. This capital would also provide wages to maintain workers during the period of production before their coordinated efforts were brought to fruition and sold on the market.

The source of this capital accumulation was, of course, the profits of production. As long as demand was brisk and more could be sold than was being produced, capitalists would invest their profits in order to expand their capital, which would lead to an increasingly intricate division of labor. The increased division of labor would lead to greater productivity, higher wages, higher profits, more capital accumulation, and so forth, in a never-ending, upward-moving escalator of social progress. The process would be brought to a halt only when there was no longer sufficient demand for the products to warrant further accumulation and more extensive division of labor. Government regulation of economic affairs, or any restrictions on the freedom of market behavior, could only decrease the extent of demand and bring the beneficial process of capital accumulation to a halt before it would have ended otherwise. So, here again, there was no room for paternalistic government meddling in economic affairs.

the theory of population

Thomas Robert Malthus' population theory was an important and integral part of classical liberal economic and social doctrines. He believed that most men were driven by an insatiable desire for sexual pleasure, and that consequently, natural rates of human reproduction, *when unchecked,* would lead to geometrical increases in population —that is, population would increase each generation at the ratio of 1, 2, 4, 8, 16, and so forth. But, food production, at the very best, increases at an arithmetical rate—that is, it can only increase each generation at a rate such as 1, 2, 3, 4, 5, and so on.

Obviously, something would have to hold the population in check. The food supply could not support a population that was growing at a geometrical rate. Malthus believed there were two general kinds of checks that limited population growth: preventive checks and positive checks. Preventive checks reduced the birth rate, whereas positive checks increased the death rate.

Moral restraint, vice, and birth control were the primary preventive checks. Moral restraint was the means by which the higher ranks of men limited their family size in order not to dissipate their wealth among larger and larger numbers of heirs. For the lower ranks of men, vice and birth control were the preventive checks, but they were grossly insufficient to curb the vast numbers of the poor.

Famine, misery, plague, and war were the positive checks. The fact that preventive checks did not succeed in limiting the numbers of lower-class people made these positive checks inevitable. Finally, if the positive checks were somehow overcome, the growing population would press upon the food supply until starvation—the ultimate and unavoidable check—succeeded in holding the population down.

Before starvation set in, Malthus advised that steps be taken to help the positive checks do their work:

> It is an evident truth that, whatever may be the rate of increase in the means of subsistence, the increase in population must be limited by it, at least after the food has once been divided into the smallest shares that will support life. All the children born, beyond what would be required to keep up the population to this level, must necessarily perish, unless room be made for them by the deaths of grown persons. . . . To act consistently therefore, we should facilitate, instead of foolishly and vainly, endeavouring to impede, the operation of nature in producing this mortality; and if we dread the too frequent visitation of the horrid form of famine, we should sedulously encourage the other forms of destruction, which we compel nature to use. Instead of recommending cleanliness to the poor, we should encourage contrary habits. In our towns we should make the streets narrower, crowd more people into the houses, and court the return of the plague. In the country, we should build our villages near stagnant pools, and particularly encourage settlements in all marshy and unwholesome situations. But above all, we should reprobate specific remedies for ravaging diseases; and those benevolent, but much mistaken men, who have thought they were doing a service to mankind by projecting schemes for the total extirpation of particular disorders. If by these and similar means the annual mortality were increased . . . we might probably every one of us marry at the age of puberty, and yet few be absolutely starved.[15]

[15] Thomas Robert Malthus, *Essay on the Principle of Population,* vol. 2 (New York: Dutton, 1961), pp. 179–180.

The masses of men, in Malthus' opinion, were incapable of exercising moral restraint, which was the only real remedy for the population problem. They were, therefore, doomed to live perpetually at a bare minimum subsistence level. If all income and wealth were distributed among them, it would be totally dissipated within one generation because of profligate behavior and population growth, and they would be as poor and destitute as ever.

Paternalistic attempts to aid the poor were, thus, doomed to failure. Furthermore, they were a positive evil because they drained wealth and income from the higher (more moral) ranks of men. These higher-class individuals were responsible, either in person or by supporting others, for all the great achievements of society. Art, music, philosophy, literature, and the other splendid cultural attainments of Western civilization owed their existence to the good taste and generosity of the higher classes of men. Taking money from them would dry up the source of such achievement; using the money to alleviate the conditions of the poor was a futile foredoomed exercise.

It is obvious that the Malthusian population theory and the liberal economic theories led to the same conclusion: Paternalistic government should avoid any attempt to intervene in the economy on behalf of the poor.

the political creed

The economic and population doctrines of classical liberalism gave rise quite naturally to a political creed that rejected the state, or government, as an evil to be tolerated only when it was the sole means of avoiding a worse evil. Much of this antipathy stemmed directly from the many corrupt, despotic, capricious, and tyrannical actions of several European kings, as well as from the actions of the English Parliament, which was notoriously unrespresentative and often despotic. The liberal creed was not put forward as an objection against particular governments, however, but against governments in general. Thomas Paine reflected the sentiment of classical liberals when he wrote: "Society in every state is a blessing, but government, even in its best state, is but a necessary evil; in its worst state an intolerable one. . . ."[16]

What were the functions that classical liberals thought should be given to governments? In *The Wealth of Nations,* Adam Smith listed three: the protection of the country against foreign invaders, the

[16] Quoted in Girvetz, op. cit., p. 66.

protection of citizens against "injustices" suffered at the hands of other citizens, and the "duty . . . of erecting and maintaining those public institutions and those public works, which, though they may be in the highest degree advantageous to a great society, are, however, of such a nature, that the profit could never repay the expense to any individual or small number of individuals, and which it therefore cannot be expected that any individual or small number of individuals should erect and maintain."[17]

This list is very general, and almost any kind of government action could be justified under one of these three functions. In order to understand the specific functions the liberals believed government should have, it is necessary to deal first with an objection that is frequently raised when the writings of Adam Smith are said to comprise a part of an ideology justifying capitalism. It is often pointed out that not only was Smith *not* a spokesman for the capitalists of his day, but also that many of his passages show that he was in general suspicious and distrustful of capitalists.[18] This contention is certainly true. Nevertheless, capitalists used the arguments put forward by Smith to justify their attempts to eliminate the last vestiges of paternalistic government when these stood in the way of their quest for profits. It was Smith's rationale that enabled them to quiet their consciences when their actions created widespread hardship and suffering. After all, they were only following his advice and pursuing their own profits; and this was the way in which they should act if they wished to be of the greatest service to society.

Finally, most classical liberals interpreted Smith's theory of the three general governmental functions in a way that showed they were not hesitant about endorsing a paternalistic government when they, the capitalists, were the beneficiaries of the paternalism. Thus, "the original doctrine of laissez faire . . . passed, for the most part, from the care of intellectuals like Adam Smith . . . into the custodianship of businessmen and industrialists and their hired spokesmen."[19]

First, the requirement that the government protect the country from external threats was often extended in the late nineteenth century to a protection or even enlargement of foreign markets through armed coercion. Second, protection of citizens against "injustices" committed by other citizens was usually defined to mean the protection of private property, the enforcement of contracts, and

17 Smith, op. cit., p. 681.

18 For a statement of this view, as well as a scholarly inquiry into classical economics from a viewpoint that differs from the one presented in this book, see Lionel Robbins, *The Theory of Economic Policy in English Classical Political Economy* (London: Macmillan, 1953).

19 Girvetz, op. cit., p. 81.

the preservation of internal order. Protection of private property, especially ownership of factories and capital equipment, is, of course, tantamount to protection of that which is the sine qua non of capitalism. It was their ownership of the means of production that gave the capitalists their economic and political power. Giving the government the function of protecting property relations meant giving the government the job of protecting the source of power of the economically and politically dominant class: the capitalists.

Contract enforcement was also essential for the successful functioning of capitalism. The complex division of labor and the necessity of complex organizing and coordinating in production, as well as the colossal size of capital investments necessary in many commercial ventures, meant that capitalists had to be able to depend on people meeting contractual commitments. The medieval notion that custom and the special circumstances of a case defined an individual's obligations was just not compatible with capitalism. Therefore, the duty to enforce contracts amounted to governmental coercion of a type necessary for capitalism to function.

The preservation of internal order was (and is) always necessary. In the late eighteenth and early nineteenth centuries, however, it often meant brutally crushing labor-union movements or the English Chartist movement, which capitalists considered to be threats to their profit-making.

Finally, the function of "erecting and maintaining those public institutions and those public works" that were in the public interest generally was interpreted to mean the creation and maintenance of institutions that fostered profitable production and exchange. These included the provision of a stable and uniform currency, standard weights and measures, and the physical means necessary for conducting business. Roads, canals, harbors, railroads, the postal services, and other forms of communication were among the prerequisites of business. Although these were often privately owned, most capitalist governments were extensively involved in their erection and maintenance either through financial subsidies to private businesses or through the direct undertaking of these projects by the governments.

Thus, it may be concluded that the classical liberals' philosophy of laissez faire was opposed to government interference in economic affairs *only if* such interference was harmful to the interests of capitalists. They welcomed and even fought for those paternalistic interferences in economic affairs that stabilized business or made larger profits possible.[20]

[20] Considerable evidence for this assertion can be found in Warren J. Samuels, *The Classical Theory of Economic Policy* (New York: World Publishing, 1966).

classical liberalism and industrialization

The industrial revolution and the triumph of the classical liberal capitalist ideology occurred together during the late eighteenth and early nineteenth centuries. Liberalism was the philosophy of the new industrial capitalism, and the new liberal ideas created a political and intellectual atmosphere in eighteenth-century England that fostered the growth of the factory system.

In its medieval version, the paternalistic Christian corporate ethic had led to a pervasive system of restrictions on the behavior of capitalists during the mercantilist period. Capitalists and their spokesmen opposed most of these restrictions with a new individualistic philosophy which advocated greater freedom for the capitalist to seek profits in a market free of encumbrances and restrictions. It is not surprising that the triumph of this philosophy should coincide with the greatest achievement of the capitalist class: the industrial revolution. The industrial revolution vaulted the capitalist class into a position of economic and political dominance, and this fact goes far in explaining the triumph of classical liberalism as the ideology of the new age of industrial capitalism.

summary

The pressure of rapidly increasing demand, and the prospect of larger profits, led to a "veritable outburst of inventive activity" in the late eighteenth and early nineteenth centuries. This period of widespread innovation—the industrial revolution—transformed England (and later western Europe and North America) into urban societies dominated by great manufacturing cities in which large numbers of workers were subjected to the dehumanizing discipline of factory production.

During this period, the classical liberal ideology of capitalism came to dominate social and economic thinking. The new ideology pictured individuals as egoistic, intellectualistic, lazy, and generally existentially independent of the society of which they were a part. Adam Smith's analysis of the market as an "invisible hand" that channeled egoistic drives into the most socially useful activities supported a doctrine of laissez faire. The only functions that this philosophy assigned to the government were those that would support and encourage profit-making.

Finally, the Malthusian theory of population taught that social action designed to mitigate the suffering of the poor was not only useless, but even had socially deleterious effects. Acceptance of this view necessitated the complete abandonment of the Christian corporate ethic.

chapter 5
socialist protest amid the industrial revolution

The industrial revolution brought about increases in human productivity that were without precedent in history. The widespread construction of factories and the extensive use of machinery represented the mechanical basis of this increase. In order to channel the economy's productivity capacity into the creation of capital goods, however, it was necessary to devote a relatively much smaller part of this capacity to the manufacture of consumer goods. Capital goods had to be purchased at a social cost of mass deprivation.

the social costs of the industrial revolution

Historically, in all cases where society has had to force a bare subsistence existence on some of its members, it has always been those with the least economic and political power who have made the sacrifices. And so it was in the industrial revolution in England. The working class lived at near the subsistence level in 1750, and their standard of living (measured in terms of the purchasing power of wages) deteriorated during the last half of the eighteenth century. The trend of working-class living standards in the first several decades of the nineteenth century is a subject of dispute among historians. The fact that many eminent scholars find sufficient evidence to argue that the living standard failed to increase, or even decreased, leads to the conclusion that any increase during this period was slight at best.

Throughout the period of the industrial revolution, there is no doubt that the standard of living of the poor fell precipitously in relative terms. A detailed analysis shows that "relatively the poor grew poorer, simply because the country, and its rich and middle class, so obviously grew wealthier. The very moment when the poor were at the end of their tether . . . was the moment when the middle class dripped with excess capital, to be wildly invested in railways and spent on the bulging opulent household furnishings displayed at the Great Exhibition of 1851, and on palatial municipal constructions . . . in the smoky northern cities."[1] There can be no doubt about which class paid the social costs in terms of the sacrificed consumption that was necessary for industrialization.

Yet the costs in terms of decreased consumption were by no means the only, and perhaps not even the worst, hardships forced upon the laboring class by the industrial revolution. The new factory system completely destroyed the laborers' traditional way of life, throwing them into a nightmare world with which they were completely unprepared to cope. They lost the pride of workmanship and close personal relationships that had existed in handicraft industries. Under the new system, their only relationship with their employer was through the impersonal market, or *cash nexus.* They lost any direct access to the means of production and were reduced to mere sellers of labor power totally dependent upon market conditions for their livelihood.

Perhaps worse than any of these was the monotonous, mechanical regularity imposed upon the worker by the factory system. In pre-industrial Europe, the worker's tasks were not so specialized. He went from one task to another, and his work was interrupted by variations in the seasons or the weather. When he felt like resting or playing or changing the pace of his work routine, he had a certain amount of freedom to do so. Factory employment brought the tyranny of the clock. Production was mechanized. Absolute regularity was necessary to coordinate the complex interaction of processes and to maximize the use of the new, expensive machinery. The pace of work was no longer decided by the man, but by the machine.

The machine, which had formerly been an appendage to the man, was now the focal point of the productive process. Man became a mere appendage to the cold, implacable, pacesetting machine.

[1] E. J. Hobsbawm, *Industry and Empire: An Economic History of Britain Since 1750* (London: Weidenfeld & Nicolson, 1968), p. 72. Several of Hobsbawm's ideas appear in this chapter.

During the late eighteenth and early nineteenth centuries, a spontaneous revolt against the new factory system saw bands of workers smashing and destroying machines and factories, which they believed were responsible for their plight. These revolts, called the Luddite revolts, ended in 1813 when large numbers of workers were hanged or deported for their activities.

The extensive division of labor in the factory made much of the work so routine and simple that untrained women and children could do it as well as men. Because women and children could be hired for much lower wages than men, and because in many cases entire families had to work in order to earn enough to eat, women and children were employed widely. Many factory owners preferred women and children because they were weaker and could be reduced to a state of passive obedience more easily than men.

Children were bound to factories by indentures of apprenticeship for seven years or until they were twenty-one. In these cases, almost nothing was given the children in return for long hours of work under the most horrendous conditions. Poor-law authorities could indenture the children of paupers. This led to "regular bargains . . . [where] children . . . were dealt with as mere merchandise . . . between the spinners on the one hand and the Poor Law authorities on the other. Lots of fifty, eighty or a hundred children were supplied and sent like cattle to the factory, where they remained imprisoned for many years."[2]

These children endured the cruelest servitude. They were totally isolated from anyone who might take pity on them and were thus at the mercy of the capitalists or their hired managers, whose main concern was the challenge of competitive factories. The children's workday was from 14 to 18 hours or until they dropped from complete exhaustion. The foremen were paid according to how much the children produced and therefore pushed them mercilessly. In most factories, the children had hardly more than 20 minutes a day for their main (and often only) meal. "Accidents were very common, especially towards the end of the overlong day, when the exhausted children almost fell asleep at their work. The tale never ended of fingers cut off and limbs crushed in the wheels."[3] The children were disciplined in such savage and brutal ways that a recitation of the methods used would appear completely incredible to the reader of today.

Women were mistreated almost as badly. Work in a factory was long, arduous, and monotonous. Discipline was harsh. Many times the price of factory employment was submission to the sexual advances

[2] Paul Mantoux, *The Industrial Revolution in the Eighteenth Century* (New York: Harcourt Brace Jovanovich, 1927), pp. 410–411.

[3] Ibid., p. 413.

of employers and foremen.[4] Women in the mines toiled 14 to 16 hours a day, stripped naked to the waist, working with men and doing the work of men. There were reports of women who came out of the mines to bear children and who were back in the mines within days after the births. Many accounts have been written of the fantastically cruel and dehumanizing working conditions for women during this period. And, of course, the working men were not much better off than the women or the children. Our sympathies are perhaps more deeply touched by narratives of the depredations suffered by women and children, but industrialization was stern, harsh, and cruel in the extreme for men as well.

Another important consideration in assessing the living standard of the working class during the period of capitalist industrialization was the rapid urbanization that took place. In 1750, only 2 cities in Britain had populations of 50,000 persons. In 1850, there were 29. By this latter date, nearly one person in three lived in a city with over 50,000 inhabitants.

Conditions in the cities of this period were terrible:

> And what cities! It was not merely that smoke hung over them and filth impregnated them, that the elementary public services—water-supply, sanitation, street-cleaning, open spaces, etc.—could not keep pace with the mass migration of men into the cities, thus producing, especially after 1830, epidemics of cholera, typhoid and an appalling constant toll of the two great groups of nineteenth-century urban killers—air pollution and water pollution, or respiratory and intestinal disease. . . . The new city populations . . . [were] pressed into overcrowded and bleak slums, whose very sight froze the heart of the observer. "Civilization works its miracles" wrote the great French liberal de Tocqueville of Manchester, "and civilized man is turned back almost into a savage."[5]

Included in these slums was a district of Glasgow that, according to a report of a government commissioner, housed

> a fluctuating population of between 15,000 and 30,000 persons. This district is composed of many narrow streets and square courts and in the middle of each court there is a dunghill. Although the outward appearance of these places was revolting, I was nevertheless quite unprepared for the filth and misery that were to be found inside. In some bedrooms we visited at night, we found a whole mass of humanity stretched on the floor. There were often 15 to 20 men and women huddled together, some

[4] Ibid., p. 416.

[5] Hobsbawm, op. cit., pp. 67–68.

being clothed and others naked. There was hardly any furniture there and the only thing which gave these holes the appearance of a dwelling was fire burning on the hearth. Thieving and prostitution are the main sources of income of these people.[6]

The total destruction of the laborers' traditional way of life and the harsh discipline of the new factory system, combined with deplorable living conditions in the cities, generated social, economic, and political unrest. Chain reactions of social upheaval, riots, and rebellion occurred in the years 1811–1813, 1815–1817, 1819, 1826, 1829–1835, 1838–1842, 1843–1844, and 1846–1848. In many areas, these were purely spontaneous and primarily economic in character. In 1816, one rioter from the Fens exclaimed: "Here I am between Earth and Sky, so help me God. I would sooner lose my life than go home as I am. Bread I want and bread I will have."[7] In 1845, an American named Colman reported that the working people of Manchester were "wretched, defrauded, oppressed, crushed human nature lying in bleeding fragments all over the face of society."[8]

There can be no doubt that industrial capitalism was erected on the base of the wretched suffering of a laboring class denied access to the fruits of the rapidly expanding economy and subjected to the most degrading of excesses to increase the capitalists' profits. The basic cause of the great evils of this period was "the absolute and uncontrolled power of the capitalist. In this, the heroic age of great undertakings, it was acknowledged, admitted and even proclaimed with brutal candor. It was the employer's own business, he did as he chose and did not consider that any other justification of his conduct was necessary. He owed his employees wages and once those were paid the men had no further claim on him."[9]

liberal social legislation

From the earliest introduction of factory production in the textile industries, workmen tried to band together to protect their interests collectively. In 1787, during a period of high unemployment, the Glasgow muslin manufacturers attempted to lower the piece rates they were paying. The workers resisted collectively, refused to work below a certain minimum rate, and organized a boycott of those

[6] Quoted in F. Engels, *The Condition of the Working Class in England in 1844* (New York: Macmillan, 1958), p. 46.

[7] Quoted in Hobsbawm, op. cit., p. 74.

[8] Ibid., p. 75.

[9] Mantoux, op. cit., p. 417.

manufacturers who would not pay the minimum rate. The struggle led to open rioting and shooting, but the workingmen proved to have a strong and well-disciplined group, and they built a strong union. In 1792, a union of weavers forced a collective agreement upon Bolton and Bury Manufacturers.

Labor organizations spread rapidly in the 1790s. As a result of this and the concurrent growth of social and economic discontent, the upper classes became very uneasy. The memory of the French Revolution was fresh in their minds, and they feared the power of united workingmen. The result was the Combination Act of 1799, which outlawed any combination of workers whose purpose was to obtain higher wages, shorter hours, or the introduction of any regulation constraining the free action of their employers. Proponents couched their arguments in terms of the necessity of free competition and the evils of monopolies—cardinal tenets of classical liberalism—but did not mention combinations of employers or monopolistic practices of capitalists. The effects of this legislation have been summarized as follows:

> The Combination Laws were considered as absolutely necessary to prevent ruinous extortions of workmen, which, if not thus restrained, would destroy the whole of the trade, manufactures, commerce and agriculture of the nation. . . . So thoroughly was this false notion entertained, that whenever men were prosecuted to conviction for having combined to regulate their wages or the hours of working, however heavy the sentence passed upon them was, and however rigorously it was inflicted, not the slightest feeling of compassion was manifested by anybody for the unfortunate sufferers. Justice was entirely out of the question: They could seldom obtain a hearing before a magistrate, never without impatience or insult . . . could an accurate account be given of proceedings, of hearings before magistrates, trials at sessions and in the Court of King's Bench, the gross injustice, the foul invective, and terrible punishments inflicted would not, after a few years have passed away, be credited to any but the best evidence.[10]

Another cause for which the classical liberals campaigned vigorously was the abolition of the Speenhamland system of poor relief that had come into existence in 1795. This system was (continuing in the tradition of the Elizabethan Statute of Artificers) the result of the paternalistic tradition of the Christian corporate ethic. It held that unfortunates would be entitled to a certain minimum living standard whether employed or not. To be sure, the system had serious

[10] Quoted in ibid., p. 449.

drawbacks: It actually depressed wages below the relief level in many cases (with the parish taxes making up the difference), and severely limited labor mobility at a time when greater mobility was needed.

The important issue, however, is not the deficiencies of the Speenhamland system, but rather the type of legislation the liberals enacted in its place when they succeeded in abolishing it in 1834. The view of the classical liberals was that workers should accept any job the market offered, regardless of the conditions or pay involved. Any person who would not or could not do so should be given just enough to prevent physical starvation. His dole should be substantially lower than the lowest wage offered in the market, and his general situation should stigmatize him sufficiently to motivate him to seek gainful employment. Thus, the new law

> was an engine of degradation and oppression more than a means of material relief. There have been few more inhuman statutes than the Poor Law Act of 1834, which made all relief "less eligible" than the lowest wage outside, confined it to the jail-like workhouse, forcibly separated husbands, wives and children in order to punish the poor for their destitution, and discourage them from the dangerous temptation of procreating further paupers.[11]

the paternalism of the tory radicals

It might seem from this discussion that the paternalism of the Christian corporate ethic was completely eclipsed during the industrial revolution. This was not so. Among the landed or aristocratic wealthy there were many Tory radicals, men who often had a "gentleman's disdain" for the "vulgar, money grubbing" middle-class merchants and manufacturers. They asserted that it was the obligation of the "higher classes" to think for and protect the poor. Some of the most vivid descriptions and outspoken denunciations of the excesses of the factory managers came from the pens of Tory radicals.

The ideas of the traditionalist Tories were summarized by John Stuart Mill (who was critical of the point of view he was summarizing). According to Mill, the traditionalists believed that

> the lot of the poor, in all things which affect them collectively, should be regulated *for* them, not *by* them. They should not be required or encouraged to think for themselves, or give to their

11 Hobsbawm, op. cit., pp. 69–70.

> own reflection or forecast an influential voice in the determination of their destiny. It is supposed to be the duty of the higher classes to think for them, and to take the responsibility of their lot, as the commander and officers of an army take that of the soldiers composing it. This function, it is contended, the higher classes should prepare themselves to perform conscientiously, and their whole demeanour should impress the poor with a reliance on it, in order that, while yielding passive and active obedience to the rules prescribed for them, they may resign themselves in all other respects to a trustful *insouciance,* and repose under the shadow of their protectors. The relationship between the rich and poor, according to this theory should be only partly authoritative; it should be amiable, moral and sentimental: affectionate tutelage on the one side, respectful and grateful deference on the other.[12]

Most of these traditionalists believed that the greedy profit-seeking of the vulgar, unrefined, acquisitive middle classes was responsible for the social ills of the industrial revolution. Capitalism would function properly, in their opinion, only when capitalists functioned as gentlemen rather than moneygrubbers. These ideas were put into practice in several industrial enterprises owned either by the aristocracy or by humane middle-class capitalists with traditionalist views. Perhaps the most famous of the latter was Robert Owen.

Born in 1771, Owen served as a draper's apprentice from the age of ten. At twenty, he was the manager of a large mill. Wise business decisions and good luck soon resulted in the acquisition of a considerable fortune. Owen was a perfect example of a benevolent autocrat. His factory at New Lanark became known throughout all England because he insisted on decent working conditions, livable wages, and education for working-class children. His workers received "affectionate tutelage" from him, and he thought of himself as their trustee and steward.

This paternalistic attitude did *not* interfere with Owen's very strict organizational discipline in his factory. Owen has described one of his methods of maintaining discipline:

> that which I found to be the most efficient check upon inferior conduct was the contrivance of a silent monitor for each one employed in the establishment. This consisted of a four-sided piece of wood, about two inches long and one broad, each side colored—one side black, another blue, the third yellow, and the fourth white, tapered at the top, and finished with wire eyes, to hang upon a hook with either side to the front. One of these

[12] John Stuart Mill, *Principles of Political Economy* (New York: Augustus M. Kelley, 1965 [first published in 1848]), p. 753.

> was suspended in a conspicuous place near to each of the persons employed, and the color at the front told the conduct of the individual during the preceding day, to four degrees of comparison. Bad, denoted by black and No. 4; indifferent by blue, and No. 3; good by yellow, and No. 2; and excellent by white, and No. 1. Then books of character were provided, for each department, in which the name of each one employed in it was inserted in the front of succeeding columns, which sufficed to mark by the number the daily conduct, day by day, for two months; and these books were changed six times a year, and were preserved; by which arrangement I had the conduct of each registered to four degrees of comparison during every day of the week, Sundays excepted, for every year they remained in my employment.[13]

So in his life and deeds, Owen, like other capitalists of his era, strove to maximize his profits. He believed that his competitors' harsh treatment of their workers was stupid and shortsighted, and he based his life on the assumption that the paternalism of the Christian corporate ethic was compatible with the capitalist system, at least at the factory level. In his own words: "My time, from early to late, and my mind, were continually occupied in devising measures and directing their execution, to improve the condition of the people, and to advance at the same time the works and the machinery as a manufacturing establishment."[14]

the socialist version of the christian corporate ethic

Although Owen's life and actions did not differentiate him from many of the conservative Tory radicals of his time, some of his ideas did. He did not believe that any society in which one class was elevated to a position of power and used this power to exploit the lower classes could ultimately become a truly good society. Private ownership of the means of production (factories, machinery, tools) was the social institution by which one small class in the existing economic system gained immense power over the mass of farmers and workers. The profit motive was the force that drove this small class to use this power to exploit the workers and farmers to gain profits.

Owen believed that in an ideal society, the people could most

13 M. Beer, ed., *Life of Robert Owen* (New York: Knopf, 1920), p. 111.

14 Ibid., p. 112.

effectively control nature, because they would reap the greatest collective benefit if they cooperated. This cooperation should take the form of self-governing industrial and agricultural communities. In such communities, private ownership of the means of production would be abolished and the selfish quest for profits would be eliminated. He maintained that only when such a society was established would it be true that

> One portion of mankind will not, as now, be trained and placed to oppress, by force or fraud, another portion, to the great disadvantage of both; neither will one portion be trained in idleness, to live in luxury on the industry of those whom they oppress, while the latter are made to labor daily and to live in poverty. Nor yet will some be trained to force falsehood into the human mind and be paid extravagantly for so doing while other parties are prevented from teaching the truth, or severely punished if they make the attempt.[15]

There was something in these writings that differed very radically from his description of the way in which he ran his own factory at New Lanark. The ideal society, for Owen, would be one in which the paternalism of the traditional Christian ethic would be expressed as a *brotherhood of equals,* a considerable shift from the parent–child type of subordination expressed in the medieval and Tory radical versions of the Christian corporate ethic.

The feudal version of the ethic had accepted a hierarchical society. In it, those at the top lived lavishly (by standards of the day, at least), and they did so by exploiting those at the bottom. Chaucer's parson's description of the medieval view is apt: "God has ordained that some folk should be more high in estate and degree and some folk more low, and that everyone should be served in his estate and his degree."[16] This traditional feudal ethic seemed to most capitalists to be incompatible with the capitalist order, and it was gradually replaced by the new individualist philosophy of classical liberalism.

Classical liberalism, however, was a two-edged sword. It became an ideology justifying the new capitalist order (see Chapter 4). But the individualistic assumptions of classical liberalism were very radical. If the old feudal aristocracy had no inherent superiority over the middle class, and if any member of the middle class was to be freed of the old restraints, and if each individual should be the best judge in deciding his own affairs, then how could one stop short of

[15] Robert Owen, "The Book of the New Moral World," reprinted in part in Carl Cohen, ed., *Communism, Fascism and Democracy* (New York: Random House, 1962), pp. 47–48.

[16] Quoted in J. L. and Barbara Hammond, *The Rise of Modern Industry* (New York: Harper & Row, Torchbooks, 1969), p. 215.

asserting the same rights and advantages for the lowest classes? The ideal that each individual ought, in some abstract way, to be considered as important as any other individual was radical indeed.

If individualism seemed to imply equality in theory, however, it certainly did not lead to it in practice. The rugged battles for more profits led not only to the social misery described above but also to a new class division of society, which was as sharply defined and as exploitative in nature as the medieval class structure. Membership in the higher class of the new system depended not on genealogy but on ownership. Capitalists derived their income and their power from the ownership of the means of production.

Socialism, then, was a protest against the inequalities of capitalism and the social evils resulting from these inequalities. The inequalities themselves, in the opinion of socialists from the earliest times to the present, resulted inevitably from the institution of private property in the means of production. Hence, socialism asserted as its most cardinal tenet that social justice demanded the abolition of private ownership of capital.

Intellectually, socialism was a wedding of the liberal notion of the equality of all men to the notion inherent in the traditional Christian corporate ethic that every man should be his brother's keeper. Incorporating the egalitarian elements of classical liberalism into the traditional Christian ethic made this a utopian ethic, in comparison with which existing society was criticized. Without this egalitarian element, the Christian ethic served well as an ideological justification of the hierarchical class system of the Middle Ages and was sometimes used to defend the capitalist system, particularly in the late nineteenth and twentieth centuries (of which more will be said later).

important pre-marxist socialists

When Owen asserted that in the ideal society, private property and acquisitive profit-seeking would be eliminated, he became part of a socialist tradition that had already been firmly established by his time. One of the first voices of socialist protest against capitalist property relations was that of Gerrard Winstanley (1609–1652), a cloth merchant who had been bankrupted in the depression of 1643. He blamed his own misfortune as well as that of others on the "cheating art of buying and selling."[17] In 1649, he led a strange band of followers from London to Saint George's Hill, Surrey. There they

[17] Quoted in Lee Cameron McDonald, *Western Political Theory: The Modern Age* (New York: Harcourt Brace Jovanovich, 1962), p. 63.

occupied unused crown lands, which they cultivated in common and, in general, shared a communal existence.

In that same year, Winstanley published *The True Levellers Standard Advanced,* in which he rebuked "the powers of England" and "the powers of the world" for their failure to realize that "the great creator . . . made the Earth a common treasury for beasts and man."[18] He asserted that all those who derived their incomes in part or in full from property ownership were violating God's commandment "Thou shalt not steal." "You pharaohs, you have rich clothing and full bellies, you have your honors and your ease; but know the day of judgment is begun and that it will reach you ere long. The poor people you oppress shall be the saviours of the land."[19]

Throughout the eighteenth and nineteenth centuries, a large number of writers argued that private property was the source of the inequities and exploitation that existed in the capitalist economy. In this chapter, we can mention only a few of the better known among them. One of the most interesting was the Frenchman Gracchus Babeuf (1760–1797). Babeuf argued that nature had made all men equal in rights and needs. Therefore, the inequalities of wealth and power that had developed should be redressed by society. Unfortunately, most societies did the opposite: They set up a coercive mechanism to protect the interests of the property holders and the wealthy. For Babeuf, the presence of inequality meant, of necessity, the presence of injustice. Capitalist commerce existed, he said, "for the purpose of pumping the sweat and blood of more or less everybody, in order to form lakes of gold for the benefit of the few."[20] The workers who created the wealth of society got the least, and until private property was eliminated, the inequalities in society could never be redressed.

Babeuf led the extreme left wing of the French revolutionary movement. After the fall of Robespierre, he masterminded a conspiracy to destroy the French government and replace it with one dedicated to equality and brotherhood. The plot was betrayed by Georges Grisel, and its leaders were arrested. Babeuf and his lieutenant, Darthe, were condemned to death and executed on February 24, 1797.

Babeuf is important in the socialist tradition because he was the first to advance the notion that if an egalitarian socialist state is to be achieved, the existing government must be toppled by force. The issue of whether socialism can be achieved peacefully has divided

[18] Ibid.

[19] Ibid.

[20] Alexander Gray, *The Socialist Tradition* (London: Longmans, Green, 1963), p. 105.

socialists since Babeuf's time. Babeuf also believed that if his revolt were successful, a period of dictatorship during the transition from capitalism to the communist democracy he envisioned would be necessary to extirpate the surviving remnants of the capitalist system. Thus, in several important ways Babeuf was a precursor of the twentieth-century Russian Bolsheviks.

Other important ideas in the socialist critique of capitalism can be seen in the writings of the Englishman William Godwin (1756–1836). Whereas the classical liberals were bemoaning the natural laziness and depravity of the lower classes, Godwin argued that the defects of the working class were attributable to corrupt and unjust social institutions. The capitalist society, in Godwin's opinion, made fraud and robbery inevitable: "If every man could with perfect facility obtain the necessaries of life . . . temptation would lose its power."[21] Men could not always obtain the necessities because the laws of private property created such great inequalities in society. Justice demanded that capitalists property relations be abolished and that property belong to that person whom it would benefit most:

> To whom does any article of property, suppose a loaf of bread, justly belong? To him who most wants it, or to whom the possession of it will be most beneficial. Here are six men famished with hunger, and the loaf is, absolutely considered, capable of satisfying the cravings of them all. Who is it that has a reasonable claim to benefit by the qualities with which the loaf is endowed? They are all brothers perhaps, and the law of primogeniture bestows it exclusively to the eldest. But does justice confirm this award? The laws of different countries dispose of property in a thousand different ways; but there can be but one way which is most conformable to reason.[22]

That one way, of course, must be based upon the equality of all men. To whom could the poor turn to correct the injustices of the system? In Godwin's opinion, it most certainly would not be the government. With economic power went political power. The rich are "directly or indirectly the legislators of the state; and of consequence are perpetually reducing oppression into a system."[23] The law, then, is the means by which the rich oppress the poor, for "legislation is in almost every country grossly the favorer of the rich against the poor."[24]

These two ideas of Godwin's were to be voiced again and again by

[21] William Godwin, *An Inquiry Concerning Political Justice,* pp. 33 and 34. Quoted in Gray, op. cit., p. 119.

[22] Ibid., p. 131.

[23] Ibid., p. 119.

[24] Ibid.

nineteenth-century socialists: (1) that capitalist social and economic institutions, particularly private property relations, were the causes of the evils and suffering within the system, and (2) that the government in a capitalist system would never redress these evils because it was controlled by the capitalist class. But Godwin had an answer to this seemingly impossible situation. He believed that human reason would save society. Once men became educated about the evils of the situation, they would reason together and arrive at the only rational solution. As Godwin saw it, this solution entailed the abolition of government, the abolition of laws, and the abolition of private property. For this radical social transformation, Godwin believed that socialists could rely, primarily, on education and reason. Most subsequent socialists argued that education and reason alone were insufficient. Education, they believed, should be only a part of the larger objective of creating a mass socialist movement. The importance of education and intellectual persuasion in attaining socialist ends has remained a much-debated issue to this day.

Other important socialist ideas were advanced by Henri de Saint-Simon (1760–1825), who was actually closer to the Tory radicals than the socialists in many ways. He came from an impoverished family of nobility, and his writings show an aristocrat's disdain for the antisocial egoism of the rich capitalists.

He also condemned the idle rich who lived off the labor of the poor but contributed nothing to society's well-being:

> Suppose that France preserves all the men of genius that she possesses in the sciences, fine arts and professions, but has the misfortune to lose in the same day Monsieur the King's brother [and all of the other members of the royal household]. . . . Suppose that France loses at the same time all the great officers of the royal household, all the ministers . . . all the councillors of state, all the chief magistrates, marshals, cardinals, archbishops, bishops, vicars-general, and canons, all the prefects and subprefects, all the civil servants, and judges, and, in addition, ten thousand of the richest proprietors who live in the style of nobles.
>
> This mischance would certainly distress the French, because they are kind-hearted, and could not see with indifference the sudden disappearance of such a large number of their compatriots. But this loss of thirty thousand individuals . . . would result in no political evil for the state.[25]

Saint-Simon was the first to emphasize the efficiency of huge industrial undertakings and argued that the government should actively intervene in production, distribution, and commerce in the

[25] F. M. H. Markham, ed., *Henri Comte de Saint-Simon, Selected Writings* (Oxford: Blackwell, 1952), pp. 72–73.

interest of promoting the welfare of the masses. He sanctioned both private property and its privileges as long as they were used to promote the welfare of the masses.

Many of his followers were more radical. They wrote endless pamphlets and books exposing abuses of capitalism, attacking private property and inheritance, denouncing exploitation, and advocating government ownership and control of economic production in the interest of the general welfare. It was from Saint-Simon and his followers that socialism inherited the idea of the necessity of government administration of production and distribution in a socialist economy.

There were many other famous socialists in the first half of the nineteenth century. The Frenchman Charles Fourier popularized the idea of cooperatives (or "phalanxes," as he called them). He attempted to change society by encouraging the formation of phalanxes. His failure proved to many socialists that capitalism could not be reformed by the mere setting of examples. He was also one of the first socialists to predict that competition among capitalists would lead inevitably to monopoly:

> Among the influences tending to restrict man's industrial rights, I will mention the formation of privileged corporations which, monopolizing a given branch of industry, arbitrarily close the doors of labour against whomsoever they please. . . . Extremes meet, and the greater the extent to which anarchical competition is carried, the nearer the approach to *universal monopoly,* which is the opposite excess. . . . Monopolies, . . . operating in conjunction with the great landed interest, will reduce the middle and labouring classes to a state of commercial vassalage. . . . The small operators will be reduced to the position of mere agents, working for the mercantile coalition. We shall then see the reappearing of feudalism in an inverse order, founded on mercantile leagues, and answering to the Baronial Leagues of the Middle Ages.[26]

Fourier believed that in a capitalist economy, only one-third of the people really did socially useful work. The other two-thirds were directed, by the corruption and distortion caused by the market system, into useless occupations or were useless, wealthy parasites. He divided these wastes into four categories:

First Waste: Useless or destructive labour. (1) the army (2) the idle rich (3) ne'er-do-wells (4) sharpers (5) prostitutes (6) magistrates (7) police (8) lawyers (9) philosophical

[26] Quoted in Sydney H. Coontz, *Productive Labor and Effective Demand* (New York: Augustus M. Kelley, 1966), p. 54.

cranks (10) bureaucrats (11) spies (12) priests and clergymen.

Second Waste: Misdirected work, since society makes it repellent, and not a vehicle of man's personality, attractive to him.

(a) Deflection of the passions into greed and morbidity, instead of being utilized as society's motors.
(b) Scale of production too small to utilize labour properly.
(c) No co-operation.
(d) No control of production.
(e) No adjustment of supply to demand, except by the mechanism of the "blind" market.
(f) The family: this economic and educational unit is absurdly small.

Third Waste: Commerce dominated by middlemen. It takes a hundred men to do what society, with warehouses, distributed according to need, could do with one. A hundred men sit at counters, wasting hours waiting for someone to enter, a hundred people write inventories, etc., competitively. These hundred wasted merchants eat without producing.

Fourth Waste: Wage labour in indirect servitude; cost of class antagonisms. Since class interests are opposed, the cost keeping men divided are greater than the gains in making them co-operate.[27]

Most socialists agreed that capitalism was irrational and wasteful and that it led to extreme inequalities and, hence, was unjust and immoral. They disagreed, however, on the tactics that they should use to achieve socialism. Many famous socialists, such as Louis Blanc (1811–1882), believed that the government could be used as an instrument of reform and that socialism could be achieved through gradual, peaceful, piecemeal reform. Others, such as Auguste Blanqui (1805–1881), the pupil of Babeuf, based his ideas on the assumption that capitalism involved a constant class war between capitalists and workers. He believed that as long as capitalists occupied the position of power, which ownership of capital gave them, they would exploit the workers, and the government and laws would be weapons to be used in this exploitation. He therefore saw no hope through gradual political reform. Revolution was, for him, the only answer.

Pierre Joseph Proudhon (1809–1865), in his well-known book,

[27] Ibid., p. 55.

What is Property?, answered the question posed in the title with a slogan that made him famous: "Property is theft." He believed that property was "the mother of tyranny." The primary purpose of the state was the enforcement of property rights. Because property rights were simply sets of special privileges for the few and general restrictions and prohibitions for the masses, they involved coercion, of necessity, in their establishment and their continued enforcement. Hence, the primary function of the state was to coerce.

"Every state is a tyranny," declared Proudhon. The state was the coercive arm of the ruling class, and Proudhon advocated resistance rather than servitude: "Whoever lays a hand on me to govern me is a usurper and a tyrant. I declare him to be my enemy." There could be no justice until property relations were abolished and the state was made unnecessary:

> To be governed is to be watched over, inspected, spied on, directed, legislated, regimented, closed in, indoctrinated, preached at, controlled, assessed, evaluated, censored, commanded; all by creatures that have neither the right, nor wisdom, nor virtue. . . . To be governed means that at every move, operation, or transaction one is noted, registered, entered in a census, taxed, stamped, priced, assessed, patented, licensed, authorized, recommended, admonished, prevented, reformed, set right, corrected. Government means to be subjected to tribute, trained, ransomed, exploited, monopolized, extorted, pressured, mystified, robbed; all in the name of public utility and the general good. Then, at the first sign of resistance or word of complaint, one is repressed, fined, despised, vexed, pursued, hustled, beaten up, garroted, imprisoned, shot, machine-gunned, judged, sentenced, deported, sacrificed, sold, betrayed, and to cap it all ridiculed, mocked, outraged, and dishonored. That is government, that is its justice and its morality! . . . O human personality! How can it be that you have cowered in such subjection for sixty centuries?"[28]

Property rights were not only the source of tyranny and coercion, they were also the source of economic inequality. Whereas the amount of labor expended determined how much was produced in a capitalist society, ownership of property determined how that produce was divided. It was divided in such a way that those who produced got almost nothing of what they produced; whereas those who owned property used the laws of private ownership to "legally steal" from the workers. In Proudhon's ideal state, he rejected not only capitalist property relations but industrialization as well. Like

[28] Quoted in Daniel Guerin, *Anarchism* (New York: Monthly Review Press, 1970), pp. 15–16; the quotations in the preceding paragraph are from the same source.

Thomas Jefferson, he envisioned a golden age of small-scale agriculture and handicraft production, in which each farmer and worker owned his own capital, and no one lived through property ownership alone.

The list could be continued, but we have included most of the important pre-Marxian socialist ideas and have introduced some of the most famous socialist thinkers. Unquestionably the most influential socialist thinker was Karl Marx, and it is to a summary of his ideas that we turn in Chapter 6.

summary

The workers bore the social costs of industrialization. The new factory system reduced most of them to poor, unhealthy, dehumanized wretches. Classical liberalism was not only impervious to their plight, it even taught that the desire to improve the conditions of the poor was quixotic and doomed to failure. Two groups of thinkers, the Tory radicals and the socialists, took strong exception to this view.

The Tory radicals had a gentleman's disdain for the "vulgar, money-grubbing" middle-class merchants and manufacturers. They clung to an essentially reactionary, paternalistic version of the Christian corporate ethic—reactionary because it seemed to assume that they could ignore industrialism and go back to an earlier agrarian way of life.

The socialists protested the inequalities of capitalism. They believed that by eliminating private ownership of capital, they could create an industrial society in which every man was treated with dignity and in which the fruits of production were equitably divided.

chapter 6
socialist protest: the economics of marx

Karl Marx (1818–1883) has been the most influential of all socialists. His writings have had, and continue to have, a profound impact not only on socialist thought but also on policy decisions that affect a large percentage of the world's population. Although he worked in close collaboration with Friedrich Engels (1820–1895) and was unquestionably deeply influenced by Engels, Marx was the intellectual leader in most matters of political economy, so no attempt is made in this chapter to distinguish Engels' separate contributions.

historical materialism

Marx believed that most of the late eighteenth- and early nineteenth-century socialists were humanitarians who were rightly indignant about the harsh exploitation that accompanied early capitalism. Despite his admiration for many of them, he gave to them the derisive label "utopian socialists." He believed most of them to be quixotic utopians who hoped to transform society by appealing to the rationality and moral sensibilities of the educated class. In Marx's view, educated men were usually members of the upper classes, and thus they owed their position, prosperity, and superior knowledge and education to the privileges inherent in the capitalist system. Therefore, they would generally do everything within their power to preserve that system. The few heretics and humanitarians among them would certainly never constitute the power base from which a transition from capitalism to socialism could be effected. Yet Marx had an undying faith that such a social and economic transition would occur. This faith was not the result of his belief in the rationality and humanity of men but rather was based on an analysis of capitalism. He concluded that internal contradictions and antagonisms within the capitalist system would eventually destroy it.

Marx based his study of capitalist society on a historical approach that has been called *historical materialism.* When he looked at the mass of ideas, laws, religious beliefs, mores, moral codes, and economic and social institutions that were present in all social systems, he tried to simplify the complex cause–effect relations that existed between these many facets of social systems. Such a simplification, he believed, would enable him to focus his attention on those relationships that were most fundamental in determining a social system's overall direction of movement and change.

Although all social institutions and intellectual traditions were reciprocally related in a complex web of cause–effect relations (each affecting and in turn being affected by the other), he believed that a society's economic base, or mode of production, exerted the most powerful influence in determining the other social institutions as well as social and religious thought. The *mode of production* consisted of two elements: (1) the forces of production and (2) the relations of production. The *forces of production* included tools, factories, equipment, production skills and knowledge of the labor force, natural resources, and the general level of technology. The *relations of production* were the social relationships between men, particularly the relations of each class of men to the means of production, which included the ownership of productive facilities and the division of the fruits of productive activity. The whole economic system, or mode of production, Marx called the *base,* or *substructure.* The religions, ethics, laws, mores, and institutions of society he called the *superstructure.*

Although the mode of production and the superstructure interacted reciprocally as both cause and effect, the mode of production was the base upon which the superstructure was built. Therefore, the line of causation running from this economic base to the superstructure was much more powerful and important than the reverse line of causation. To argue that Marx believed that the economic base determined, completely and rigidly, every aspect of the superstructure is grossly inaccurate (although it is often done). He did assert, however, that the mode of production was the most important single aspect in determining not only the present social superstructure but also the direction of social change.

When he referred to the relations of production Marx meant the class structure of society, the most important single aspect of the mode of production. The antagonisms between social classes were, for Marx, the propelling force in history. "The history of all hitherto existing society is the history of class struggles."[1] he proclaimed. The importance of the mode of production and the class antagonisms it engendered have been summarized by Marx in a famous passage:

> In the social production which men carry on they enter into definite relations that are indispensable and independent of their will; these relations of production correspond to a definite stage of development of their material powers of production. The sum total of these relations of production constitutes the economic structure of society —the real foundation, on which rise legal and political superstructures and to which correspond definite forms of social consciousness. The mode of production in material life determines the general character of the social, political, and spiritual processes of life. It is not the consciousness of men that determines their existence, but, on the contrary, their social existence determines their consciousness. At a certain stage of their development, the material forces of production in society come into conflict with the existing relations of production, or—what is but a legal expression for the same thing—with the property relations within which they had been at work before. From forms of development of the forces of production these relations turn into their fetters. Then comes the period of social revolution. With the change of economic foundation the entire immense superstructure is more or less rapidly transformed. In considering such transformations the distinction should always be made between the material transformation of the economic conditions of production which can be determined with the precision of natural science, and the legal, political, religious, aesthetic, or philosophic—in short ideological forms in which men become conscious of this conflict and fight it out.[2]

Marx identified four separate economic systems, or modes of production, through which the European civilization had evolved: (1) primitive communal, (2) slave, (3) feudal, and (4) capitalist. In any one of these economic systems, there was a unique mode of production which included forces of production as well as a particular class structure, or relations of production. Increasing demands for more production inevitably led to changes in the forces of production, yet the relationships of production, or class positions, remained

1 Karl Marx and Friedrich Engels, "The Communist Manifesto," in Arthur P. Mendel, ed., *Essential Works of Marxism* (New York: Bantam, 1965), p. 13.

2 Karl Marx, *Critique of Political Economy,* reprinted in part in Howard Selsam and Harry Martel, eds., *Reader in Marxist Philosophy* (New York: International Publishers, 1963), pp. 186–187.

fixed and were fiercely defended. Therefore, there were conflicts, tensions, and contradictions between the changing forces of production and the fixed social relations (and vested interests) of production. These conflicts and contradictions grew in intensity and importance until a series of violent social eruptions destroyed the old system and created a new system which would have new class relationships compatible (for a time at least) with the changed forces of production.

In each mode of production, the contradictions that developed between the forces of production and the relations of production showed themselves in the form of a class struggle. The struggle raged between the class that controlled the means of production and received most of the benefits and privileges of the system (e.g., the Roman slaveholders) and the much-larger class that they controlled and exploited (e.g., the Roman slaves). In all economic systems prior to capitalism, this class struggle had destroyed one system only to create a new system based upon exploitation of the masses by a new ruling class, and hence the beginning of a new class struggle. Capitalism, however, was, in Marx's opinion, the last mode of production that would be based upon the existence of antagonistic classes. The capitalist class, which ruled by virtue of its ownership of the means of production, would be overthrown by the proletariat, or working class, which would establish a classless society in which the means of production were owned in common by all. The transition from capitalism to socialism will be discussed in greater detail below. Before proceeding further, however, it is necessary to examine the basis of Marx's moral condemnation of capitalism.

marx's moral critique of capitalism

According to Marx, two most important features define capitalism and distinguish it from other economic systems: (1) The separation of the worker from the means of production created a class of owners and a class of workers; (2) the market, or cash nexus, was extended into all human relationships involved in production and distribution. Like most socialists before him, Marx deplored the extremes of wealth and poverty that this class relationship created.

His moral condemnation of capitalism, however, went beyond an ethical rejection of these great inequalities. His most important criticism of capitalism involved the idea that within a capitalist system, men could not develop their innate potentialities. They could not become emotionally or intellectually fully developed men.

Man differed from animals because in order to satisfy his needs, he created tools and worked with them to shape and control his environment. Man's senses and intellect were developed and refined through working. Through his relations with what he produced, man achieved both pleasure and self-realization. In precapitalist social systems such as feudalism, man could achieve this self-realization through work despite an exploitative class structure. Because the exploitative social relations were also personal and paternalistic, work was not merely a means of making money.

This changed with capitalism, when, in Marx's opinion:

> the bourgeoisie, wherever it has got the upper hand, has put an end to all feudal patriarchal, idyllic relations. It has pitilessly torn asunder the motley feudal ties that bound man to his "natural superiors," and has left remaining no other nexus between man and man than naked self-interest, than callous "cash payment." It has drowned the most heavenly ecstasies of religious fervor, of chivalrous enthusiasm, of philistine sentimentalism, in the icy water of egotistical calculation. It has resolved personal worth into exchange value. . . .[3]

In a capitalist society, the market separated and isolated "exchange value," or money price, from the qualities that shaped man's relation with things as well as with other human beings. This was especially true in the work process. To the capitalist, wages were merely another expense of production to be added to the costs of raw materials and machinery in the profit calculation. Labor became a mere *commodity* to be bought if a profit could be made on the purchase. Whether the laborer could sell his labor power was completely beyond his control. It depended on the cold and totally impersonal conditions of the market. The product of this labor was likewise totally outside of the laborer's life, being the property of the capitalist.

Marx used the term *alienation* to describe the condition of men in this situation. They felt alienated or divorced from their work, from their institutional and cultural environment, and from their fellow men. The conditions of work, the object produced, and indeed the very possibility of working were determined by the numerically small class of capitalists and their profit calculations, not by human need or aspirations. The effects of this alienation can best be summarized in Marx's own words:

> What, then, constitutes the alienation of labour?
>
> First, the fact that labour is external to the worker, i.e., it does not belong to his essential being; that in his work, therefore, he does not affirm himself but denies himself, does not feel content but unhappy, does not develop freely his physical and mental energy but mortifies

[3] Marx and Engels, "The Communist Manifesto," op. cit., p. 15.

> his body and ruins his mind. The worker therefore only feels himself outside his work, and in his work feels outside himself. He is at home when he is not working, and when he is working he is not at home. His labour is therefore not voluntary but coerced; it is *forced labour.* It is therefore not the satisfaction of a need; it is merely a *means* to satisfy needs external to it. Its alien character emerges clearly in the fact that as soon as no physical or other compulsion exists, labour is shunned like the plague. External labour, labour in which man alienates himself, is a labour of self-sacrifice, or mortification. Lastly, the external character of labour for the worker appears in the fact that it is not his own, but someone elses, that it does not belong to him, that in it he belongs, not to himself, but to another. . . . As a result, therefore, man (the worker) no longer feels himself to be freely active in any but his animal functions—eating, drinking, procreating, or at most in his dwelling and in dressing up, etc.; and in his human functions he no longer feels himself to be anything but an animal. What is animal becomes human and what is human becomes animal.[4]

It was this degradation and total dehumanization of the working class, thwarting man's personal development and making an alien market commodity of man's life-sustaining activities, that Marx most thoroughly condemned in the capitalist system. Thus, his moral critique went far beyond those of most of his socialist precursors. His faith in the possibility of a better future for the working class, however, was not based on the hope that ever-increasing numbers of people would share his moral indignation and therefore attempt to reform the system. Rather, he believed that the capitalist mode of production and the class conflict inherent in it would lead to the destruction of capitalism. Capitalism, like all previous modes of production in which class conflicts were present, would destroy itself. In order to understand the basis for this faith, it is necessary to examine his economic theory, in which he attempted to analyze the "laws of motion" of capitalism.

the labor theory of value and surplus value

Because, for Marx, the capitalist mode of production was based upon the opposition of labor and capital, he began by analyzing the capital-labor relation. This relation was essentially one of exchange. The worker sold his labor power to the capitalist for money, with which the worker bought the necessities of life. Thus, this exchange

[4] Karl Marx, *Economic and Philosophic Manuscripts of 1844* (Moscow: Progress Publishers, 1959), p. 69.

relation was obviously merely a special case of the general problem of exchange values within a capitalist market economy. Marx, therefore, began volume 1 of *Capital* with a section entitled "Commodities" in which, he defined *commodities* as objects that are usually intended for exchange rather than for the direct personal use of the producer. He then attempted to analyze the basic determinant of the exchange value of commodities. In other words, he analyzed the ratio in which commodities could be exchanged for other commodities, as opposed to use value which was a measure of the usefulness of commodities to their possessor.

Like Adam Smith, David Ricardo (Smith's most important disciple), and most of the pre-Marxian classical economists, Marx believed that the exchange value of a commodity was determined by the amount of labor time necessary for its production. His theory is, therefore, usually called the *labor theory of value.* He recognized that laborers differed in abilities, training, and motivation, but he believed that skilled labor could be calculated as a multiple of unskilled labor. Thus, all labor time could be reduced to a common denominator: *abstract labor.*

He also realized that labor time expended in the production of a useless commodity (one for which there was no demand) would not create a commodity with an exchange value equal to the labor time embodied in it. The desire of capitalists to maximize their profits would, however, prevent the production of objects for which there was no demand. Capitalists would produce only those commodities for which market demand would permit the realization of at least their costs of production. Market demand would determine not only what commodities were produced but also the relative quantities in which they were produced.

Marx began by describing a system of *simple commodity production,* in which each producer owned his own means of production and sold the commodities he produced. The producer would exchange his commodities for money, with which he would buy other commodities for his own use. Simple commodity production was then contrasted with *capitalist commodity production,* in which the capitalist begins the process with only money. He buys the means of production and the labor power, and when the laborers complete the production process, he sells the commodities for more money. Thus, the money with which he ends is greater than that with which he started. This difference is what Marx called *surplus value.* He considered it to be the source of capitalist profits.

Surplus value originated in the fact that capitalists bought one commodity—labor power—and sold a different commodity—that which labor produced in the production process. Profits were made because the value of labor power was less than the value of the commodities produced with the labor power. The value of labor power was "determined, as in the case of every other commodity, by the labor time necessary" for its maintenance and reproduction, which meant that "the value of labor power . . . [was] the value of the means of subsistence necessary for the maintenance of the laborer at a socially defined minimal standard of living."[5] The fact was that the average length of the working day exceeded the time necessary for a laborer to produce the value-equivalent of his subsistence wage, which enabled the capitalist to appropriate the surplus produced over and above this subsistence.

the accumulation of capital

The capitalist gained his profits because of his ownership of capital. Most of these profits were plowed back to increase his capital and hence increase future profits, which could then be plowed back into more capital, and so forth. This was the process of capitalist accumulation: Capital led to profits, which led to more capital. When and how did the process originate? Many classical economists and liberals, particularly the English economist Nassau Senior (1790–1864), had answered this question in a way favorable to the capitalist, arguing that through hard, diligent work and abstemious behavior, the capitalist had begun a modest saving program, which enabled him to accumulate slowly the fortunes that many nineteenth-century capitalists owned. Laborers, on the contrary, rather than devoting themselves to working and living abstemiously, had profligately squandered their earnings.

Marx accused these defenders of the capitalist system of being totally ignorant of history. In a famous passage, which gives the flavor of some of his most colorful writing, Marx described the process of "primitive accumulation" by which the fortunes were originally made:

> This primitive accumulation plays in Political Economy about the same part as original sin in theology. Adam bit the apple, and thereupon sin fell on the human race. Its origin is supposed to be explained when it is told as an anecdote of the past. In times long gone by there were two sorts of people; one, the diligent, intelligent, and above all, frugal elite; the other, lazy rascals, spending their substance, and more, in riotous living. . . . Thus it came to pass that the former sort accumulated wealth, and the latter sort had nothing

[5] Karl Marx, *Capital,* vol. 1 (Moscow: Foreign Language Publishing House, 1961), pp. 170–171.

> to sell except their own skins. And from this original sin dates the poverty of the great majority that, despite all its labour, has up to now nothing to sell but itself, and the wealth of the few that increases constantly although they have long ceased to work. Such insipid childishness is every day preached to us in the defence of property. . . . As soon as the question of property crops up, it becomes a sacred duty to proclaim the intellectual food of the infant as the one thing fit for all ages and for all stages of development. In actual history it is notorious that conquest, enslavement, robbery, murder, briefly force, play the great part. . . . The methods of primitive accumulation are anything but idyllic.[6]

Marx listed the important forms of primitive accumulation as the enclosures and the dislocation of the feudal agrarian population, the great price inflation, monopolies of trade, colonies, "the extirpation, enslavement and entombment in mines of the aboriginal population, the beginning of the conquest and looting of the East Indies, [and] the turning of Africa into a warren for the commercial hunting of black skins."[7]

Once this initial accumulation of capital had taken place, the drive to acquire more capital became the moving force of the capitalist system. The capitalist's social standing and prestige as well as his economic and political power depended on the size of the capital he controlled. He could not stand still; he was beset on every side by fierce competition. The system demanded that he accumulate and grow more powerful in order to outdo his competitors, or else his competitors would force him to the wall and take over his capital. Competitors were constantly developing new and better methods of production. Only by accumulating new and better capital equipment could this challenge be met. Thus, Marx believed that the capitalist

> shares with the miser the passion for wealth as wealth. But that which in the miser is a mere idiosyncrasy, is in the capitalist the effect of the social mechanism of which he is but one of the wheels. Moreover, the development of capitalist production makes it constantly necessary to keep increasing the amount of capital laid out in a given industrial undertaking, and competition makes the immanent laws of capitalist production to be felt by each individual capitalist as external coercive laws. It compells him to keep constantly extending his capital, in order to preserve it, but extend it he cannot except by means of progressive accumulation.[8]

[6] Ibid., pp. 713–714.

[7] Ibid., p. 751.

[8] Ibid., p. 592.

sectoral imbalances and economic crises

It was this ceaseless drive to accumulate more capital that created many of the contradictions of capitalist development. The capitalist would begin with the acquisition of more machines and tools of the types that were currently being used. This would require a proportional increase in the number of workers employed in order to operate the new equipment. But the capitalists had been able to keep the wage rate at the subsistence level only because there existed what Marx called an "industrial reserve army" of unemployed labor, which was living at below subsistence and striving to take jobs that would pay a mere subsistence wage. Therefore capitalists usually had no problem in keeping wage rates down. As the industrial expansion took place, however, the increasing demand for labor soon depleted the ranks of the reserve. When this happened, the capitalist began to find that he had to pay higher wages to get enough labor.

The individual capitalist took the wage level as given and beyond his power to change, so he attempted to make the best of the situation. The most profitable course of action seemed to be changing the techniques of production by introducing new labor-saving machinery so that each laborer would then be working with more capital and output per laborer could be increased. This labor-saving investment would enable the capitalist to expand output with the same or an even smaller work force. When all or most of the capitalists, acting individually, did this, the problem of high wages was temporarily alleviated as the reserve army was replenished by workers displaced by the new productive techniques. The creation of technological unemployment saved the day. But not without introducing new problems and contradictions.

Labor-saving expansion permitted increases in total production without increasing the wages paid to workers. Therefore, while new goods were flooding the market, workers' wages were being restricted, with the result that consumer demand was limited. As Marx put it, the workers were still producing more profits in the form of goods, but the capitalists could not "realize" the profits by selling these goods in the market because of lack of consumer demand.

In order to clarify this process further, Marx divided the capitalist economy into two sectors, one producing consumer goods and the other producing capital goods. Lack of consumer demand meant that capitalists in the consumption-goods sector would find they could not sell their entire output and thus would lower their expectations of profits and would certainly *not* want to add to their productive facilities. They would, therefore, cancel any plans to add to their already excessively large capital stock. These decisions would, of course, significantly reduce the demand for capital goods, which would result in a decrease in production in the capital-goods sector. Unlike the naïve underconsumptionist theories of the earlier socialists, Marx noted that the first obvious sign of a depression might thus appear in the capital-goods sector.

The actual decrease in capital-goods production would mean that some workers in that sector would be fired, which would lower total wages, decrease national income, and reduce consumer demand. Thus, there would be a cutback in consumer-goods production, and layoffs of workers would spread to those industries. Wages and incomes would then be further reduced, causing a glut, or surfeit, of consumer goods. The entire process of successive repercussions in both sectors would then be one of economic collapse.

The resulting depression would more than restore the reserve army of unemployed and push labor's standard of living back to or below the subsistence level. Marx, however, was not a "stagnationist" —that is, he did not believe that capitalism would suffer one long depression or that mass unemployment at high levels would last forever. In the depression, workers' wages would fall, but not as rapidly as the output of goods. Thus, eventually supply would be lower than consumer demand, and therefore recovery would occur. Marx believed that capitalism does grow, but jerkily, in cycles of boom and bust, with periodic high levels of unemployment for the workers.

economic concentration

Concentration of wealth and economic power in the hands of fewer and fewer capitalists was another important consequence of capital accumulation. This concentration was the result of two forces. First, competition between capitalists tended to create a situation in which the strong either crushed or absorbed the weak. "Here competition rages in direct proportion to the number, and in inverse proportion to the magnitudes, of the antagonistic capitals. It always ends in the ruin of many small capitalists, whose capitals partly pass into the hands of their conquerors, partly vanish."[9]

Second, as technology improved, there was "an increase in the minimum amount of . . . capital necessary to carry on a business

[9] Ibid., p. 626.

under its normal conditions." In order to remain competitive a firm would constantly have to increase the productivity of its laborers. The "productiveness of labor . . . [depended] on the scale of production."[10] Thus, changing technology as well as competition among capitalists created an inexorable movement of the capitalist system toward larger and larger firms owned by fewer and fewer capitalists. In this way, the gulf between the small class of wealthy capitalists and the great majority of society, the proletariat, continually widened.

the immiserization of the proletariat

At the same time that this increasing concentration of capital was taking place, the misery of the proletariat grew constantly worse. In his famous "doctrine of increasing misery" (immiserization), Marx argued that the conditions of labor would worsen, relative to the affluence of the capitalists, until the laborers could stand no more. And then revolution was inevitable. Because Marx's doctrine of immiserization is very often misrepresented, we will quote his own writings on this point:

> within the capitalist system all methods for raising the social productiveness of labour are brought about at the cost of the individual labourer; all means for the development of production transform themselves into means of domination over, and exploitation of, the producers; they mutilate the labourer into a fragment of a man, degrade him to the level of an appendage of a machine, destroy every remnant of charm in his work and turn it into hated toil; they estrange from him the intellectual potentialities of the labour-process in the same proportion as science is incorporated in it as an independent power; they distort the conditions under which he works, subject him during the labour-process to a despotism the more hateful for its meanness; they transform his life time into working time, and drag his wife and child beneath the wheels of the Juggernaut of capital. But all methods for the production of surplus-value are at the same time methods of accumulation; and every extension of accumulation becomes again a means for the development of those methods. It follows therefore that in proportion as capital accumulates, the lot of the labourer, be his payment high or low, must grow worse. The law . . . establishes an accumulation of misery, corresponding with accumulation of capital. Accumulation of wealth at one pole is, therefore, at the same time accumulation of

[10] Ibid.

> misery, agony of toil, slavery, ignorance, brutality [and] mental degradation at the opposite pole. . . .[11]

It should be noted that Marx asserted that the laborer would become worse off even if his wages increased. There were two reasons for this. First, Marx believed that even if workers' wages increased, they would not increase by as much as capitalists' profits increased. The worker would, therefore, become continuously worse off, *relative* to the capitalist. Second, Marx correctly foresaw that as the capitalist system progressed, there was to be an increasingly minute division of labor.

A finer division of labor makes the worker's activities less varied, and his job becomes more repetitious and tedious. Marx agreed with Adam Smith, who had stated that "the man whose whole life is spent in performing a few simple operations . . . generally becomes as stupid and ignorant as it is possible for a human creature to become."[12] Forced into a condition of stupor, and increasingly severely alienated, "the lot of the labourer *be his payment high or low,* must grow worse."[13]

the capitalist state

Marx rejected the notion that socialism could be created through gradual, piecemeal reforms undertaken by the state. By *the state,* Marx meant something more than simply any government: ". . . we may speak of a state only where a special public power of coercion exists which, in the form of an armed organization, stands over and above the population."[14]

Many socialists believed that the state was (or could be) an impartial arbiter in the affairs of society, and they had faith in moral and intellectual appeals to the state. Marx rejected this idea. "Political power," he declared in the *Communist Manifesto,* "is merely the organized power of one class for oppressing another." During each period of history, or for each mode of production, the state is the coercive instrument of the ruling class.

Friedrich Engels has summarized the Marxist argument:

> Former society, moving in class antagonisms, had need of the state, that is, an organization of the exploiting class at each period for

[11] Ibid., p. 645.

[12] Adam Smith, *The Wealth of Nations,* ed. Andrew Skinner (London: Penguin Books, 1970), p. 80.

[13] Marx, *Capital,* op. cit., p. 645.

[14] Sidney Hook, *Towards the Understanding of Karl Marx* (New York: Day, 1933), p. 256.

> the maintenance of external conditions of production; that is, therefore, for the forcible holding down of the exploited class in the conditions of oppression (slavery, villeinage or serfdom, wage labor) determined by the existing mode of production. The state was the official representative of society as a whole, its embodiment in a visible corporation; but it was this only in so far as it was the state of that class which itself, in its epoch, represented society as a whole; in ancient times, the state of the slave-owning citizens; in the Middle Ages, of the feudal nobility; in our epoch, of the bourgeosie.[15]

Thus, the state is simply a dictatorship of the ruling class over the remainder of society.

In the capitalist system, the state has two functions. First, it has the traditional function of enforcing the dictatorship of the capitalists over the rest of society. The state achieves this, primarily, by enforcing propery rights, the source of the capitalists' economic power. It also serves in innumerable other ways—for example, jailing or harassing critics of capitalism, fighting wars to extend capitalists' markets, and providing roads, railroads, canals, postal service, and hundreds of other prerequisites for the conduct of profitable commerce. Second, the government acts as the arbiter of the rivalries between capitalists. Each capitalist is interested only in his own profits, and, therefore, it is inevitable that the interests of capitalists will clash. If not resolved, many of these clashes would threaten the very existence of the system. Thus, the government intervenes, and in doing so, it protects the viability of the capitalist system. This is why it is sometimes possible to observe the government acting in a way that is contrary to the interests of *some* of the capitalists. But the government never acts in a way that is contrary to the interests of *all* capitalists, taken as a class.

For these reasons, Marx rejected the notion that socialists could rely upon the government for help in bringing about the transition from capitalism to socialism. The establishment of socialism, in Marx's opinion, would require a revolution.

the socialist revolution

In his overall view of capitalism, Marx saw the process of capital accumulation as inevitably involving several steps. Business cycles or crises would occur regularly and with increasing severity as the capitalist economy developed. There would be a long-run tendency for the rate of profit to fall, which would exacerbate the other

15 Friedrich Engels, "Anti-Duhring," in *Handbook of Marxism* (New York: Random House, 1935), p. 295.

problems of capitalism. Industrial power would become increasingly concentrated in fewer and fewer giant monopolistic and oligopolistic firms, and wealth would become concentrated in the hands of fewer and fewer capitalists. The plight of the laborer would steadily deteriorate.

Given these increasingly bad conditions, the system could not be perpetuated. Eventually, life under capitalism would become so intolerable that workers would revolt, overthrow the whole system, and create a more rational socialist economy.

> Along with the constantly diminishing number of magnates of capital, who usurp and monopolize all advantages of this process of transformation, grows the mass of misery, oppression, slavery, degradation, exploitation; but with this too grows the revolt of the working-class, a class always increasing in numbers, and disciplined, united, organized by the very mechanism of the process of capitalist production itself. The monopoly of capital becomes a fetter upon the mode of production, which has sprung up and flourished along with, and under it. Centralization of the means of production and socialization of labour at last reach a point where they become incompatible with their capitalist integument. This integument is burst asunder. The knell of capitalist private property sounds. The expropriators are expropriated.[16]

In subsequent chapters, we shall examine the defenses of capitalism offered in opposition to Marx, as well as the further development of socialist thought after Marx.

summary

Karl Marx, the most influential of all socialists, based his economic analysis on a theory of history called historical materialism. Most social and political institutions, he believed, were significantly shaped by the economic base of society: the mode of production. Over time, conflicts developed between the forces of production and the relations of production. The working-out of these conflicts was the most important element in the historical evolution of society.

Marx's economic writings were aimed at understanding the conflicts between the class system (or private property system) of capitalism and the methods of production and commodity exchange under capitalism. The conflicts, he believed, would ultimately lead to the overthrow of capitalism and its replacement by a classless, socialist society.

16 Marx, *Capital,* op. cit., p. 763.

chapter 7
the rise of corporate capitalism and the defense of laissez faire

The period from the mid-1840s to 1873 (the year that marked the beginning of the Long Depression in Europe) has been called the golden age of competitive capitalism.[1] These were years of rapid economic expansion throughout most of Europe. Industrialization was getting under way in the United States and continental Europe. The new capital goods necessary for industrialization were, to a large extent, imported from England. Between 1840 and 1860, England experienced an expansion of her exports that was more rapid than it had ever been before or has been since that period. Capital goods increased from 11 percent of English exports to 22 percent, and exports of coal, iron, and steel also rose sharply.

Between 1830 and 1850, England experienced a railroad-building boom in which some 6,000 miles of railroads were constructed. This railroad-building created a strong demand for iron, the production of which doubled between the mid-1830s and the mid-1840s. During the next 30 years, the increases in industrial production were also very impressive. Between 1850 and 1880, the production of pig iron increased from 2,250,000 to 7,750,000 tons per year; steel production went from 49,000 to 1,440,000 tons; and coal increased by 300 percent, to 147,000,000 tons. The Bessemer converted (in the 1850s), the open-hearth furnace (in the 1860s), and the basic process (in the 1870s) completely revolutionized the steel industry, making large-

[1] Dudley Dillard, *Economic Development of the North Atlantic Community* (Englewood Cliffs, N.J.: Prentice-Hall, 1967), p. 363.

scale mass production of high-quality steel possible at much lower costs. The capital-goods industries also prospered in the last half of the nineteenth century. The production of machines, ships, chemicals, and other important capital goods employed twice as many men in 1881 as in 1851.

the concentration of corporate power

Just as competitive capitalism seemed to be achieving its greatest successes, the forces that Marx had predicted would lead to the concentration of capital began to show themselves. Improvements in technology were such that larger-sized plants were necessary to take advantage of the more efficient methods of production. Competition became so aggressive and destructive that small competitors were eliminated. Large competitors, facing mutual destruction, often combined in cartels, trusts, or mergers in order to assure their mutual survival. In the United States, this competition was particularly intense (it is described in greater detail in Chapter 8).

A factor that Marx had nearly overlooked, the revolutionary changes in transportation and communication, led to ever-widening markets that could be efficiently supplied by single companies or corporations. The joint-stock company, or corporation, became an effective means by which a single business organization could gain control over vast amounts of capital. And a large, well-organized money market evolved in Europe and North America, which successfully channeled the smaller capital holdings of many thousands of individuals and small businesses into the hands of large corporations.

In the late nineteenth-century world of giant corporations, in which articles were mass-produced for nationwide or worldwide markets, price competition (and indeed sometimes any kind of competition) proved to be so destructive that it was abandoned almost completely in the large and important industries. There was an inexorable trend toward monopoly, or at least toward collusive oligopoly, which amounted to much the same thing. Many business giants entered into voluntary combinations in which each firm remained somewhat autonomous (e.g., cartels and pools). Other combinations used a financial enterprise such as a trust or holding company to control the voting stock of the corporations involved. Still others used direct mergers and amalgamations from which a single unified corporation emerged.

THE ENGLISH CASE

England, where the classical liberal laissez faire philosophy had taken root most firmly, was perhaps least affected by this movement to corporate monopolies. Advances in technology led to a steel industry made up of very large producers. Nevertheless, the fact that England had very few restrictions on imports prevented the industry from combining into an effectively coordinated group until after the trade restrictions of 1932. The producers of some heavy steel products, such as ship and boiler plate, however, were able to create effective monopolies much earlier.

In other industries, amalgamations led to heavy concentrations. English railroads were combined very early into four main companies. Banking was consolidated until five large commercial banks dominated the industry by the time of World War I. In 1896, the five rivals in the cotton sewing-thread industry had merged into a single monopoly (J. & P. Coats), which came to dominate the entire world market for that commodity and regularly made profits of 20 percent or more. The firm of Lever Brothers, through amalgamations, gained dominance over the soap business in England as well as in several other countries. Monopolies or closely coordinated oligopolies came to control the wallpaper, salt, petroleum, and rubber industries. Many other industries were either dominated or strongly influenced by a few large firms.

THE GERMAN CASE

In Germany, the classical liberal ideology had never really taken root. During Germany's rapid rise to industrial power during the last half of the nineteenth century, there were neither philosophical nor ideological nor legal barriers to large-scale monopolistic industries. It is, therefore, not surprising that monopolies and combinations were more widespread in Germany than in any other country in Europe. The cartel was the main type of monopolistic business combination in Germany. There were approximately 16 cartels in 1879; the figure rose to 35 by 1885, to 300 by 1900, to 600 by 1911, to 1,000 by 1922, and to 2,100 by 1930.

Thus, by the early twentieth century, monopolistic cartels completely dominated almost all the important sectors of the German capitalist economy. (The legal and philosophical justifications of these monopolistic German cartels will be discussed in Chapter 8.)

THE AMERICAN CASE

In the United States, the Civil War gave a great stimulus to industrialization. The war not only increased the demand for industrially produced commodities but also led to the passage of laws that were beneficial to the newly emerging corporations which were soon to dominate American industry.

In an effort to provide civil and political rights for all Americans, Congress had passed the first Civil Rights Act in 1866. By 1868, the Fourteenth Amendment to the U.S. Constitution had been ratified by the states. The ostensible aim of these laws was to confer citizenship and equal rights on American blacks. The Civil Rights Act declared that citizens "of every race and color" were to have equal rights to make contracts, to sue, and to enjoy "full and equal benefit of all laws and proceedings for the security of person and property."[2]

Most of the Civil Rights Act was incorporated into the Fourteenth Amendment. The Amendment also included the famous due process clause, which prohibited any state government from depriving "any person of life, liberty, or *property,* without due process of law."[3]

For decades after its ratification, the Fourteenth Amendment had no effect at all on the civil rights of American blacks; many of them were thrust into situations that were worse than slavery. Rather, most court decisions based on the Fourteenth Amendment involved corporations. The courts ruled that corporations were persons and as such, were protected under the due process clause.

Each time a state government attempted to curb the extravagant excesses of corporations by passing regulatory legislation, the federal courts would invalidate the legislation because it violated the due process clause of the amendment. State governments became powerless before the growing strength of large corporations.

Representative John A. Bingham, who had written the due process clause, later admitted that he had phrased it "word for word and syllable for syllable" to protect the rights of private property and the corporations. Representative Roscoe Conkling, who had also helped frame the Amendment, later declared: "At the time the Fourteenth Amendment was ratified, individuals and *joint stock companies* were appealing for congressional and administrative protection against invidious and discriminating state and local taxes. . . . [the Fourteenth amendment embodies] the Golden Rule, so entrenched

2 Quoted in Kenneth M. Stampp. *The Era of Reconstruction, 1865–1877* (New York: Random House, Vintage Books, 1967), p. 136.

3 Ibid.; italics added.

as to curb the many who would do to the few as they would not have the few do to them."[4]

With the knowledge that they could go to almost any lengths in their pursuit of profits, without fear of state government controls, the corporations thrived. They grew through internal expansion and, more importantly, through absorbing their competitors. As the giant corporations flourished, the entire American economy thrived and grew.

By the turn of the century, the United States had become the leading industrial power in the world. By 1913, when the American economy produced over one-third of the world's industrial output—more than double that of its closest competitor, Germany—most of the strategic industries (railroads, meat-packing, banking in the large cities, steel, copper, and aluminum) and important areas of manufacturing were dominated by a relatively small number of immensely powerful corporations.

With the exception of the railroads, most industries in the immediate post-Civil War years had been relatively atomistic by present-day standards. Although accurate statistics are not available for this early period, it has been estimated that the largest 200 nonfinancial enterprises would have controlled a very minor and inconsequential percentage of all business assets. By the end of the 1920s, this had grown to 33 percent of all assets.[5]

The primary cause of this concentration was the wave of combinations and mergers that took place at an unprecedented rate during the last quarter of the nineteenth century. This merger movement was the outgrowth of the particularly severe competition that had ravaged and destroyed scores of businesses. During this period, many people began to question seriously the liberal notion of the invisible hand. It seemed to them that unrestrained individualism had led to unrestrained warfare.

> As growing giant businesses locked horns, railroad against railroad, steel mill against steel mill, each sought to assure the coverage of its fixed expenses by gaining for itself as much of the market as it could. The outcome was the steady growth of cutthroat competition among massive producers. . . . On the railroads for example, constant rate-wars were fought in the 1870s. In the oil fields, the coal fields, among the steel and copper producers, similar price-wars repeatedly broke out as producers sought to capture the markets.[6]

[4] Ibid., p. 137.

[5] Joe S. Bain, *Industrial Organization* (New York: John Wiley, 1959), pp. 191–192.

[6] Robert L. Heilbroner, *The Making of Economic Society* (Englewood Cliffs, N.J.: Prentice-Hall, 1962), p. 120.

The outcome of such competition was the destruction or absorption of the small competitors. Eventually, only giants remained, and at this point, further competition was immensely destructive to all competitors. The merger movement represented the means whereby the surviving firms could escape this competition.

> The scope of the merger movement was so great that by 1904 it had basically altered the structure of American industry. By the beginning of that year there were over three hundred large industrial combinations with a combined capitalization in excess of $7,000,000,000. They controlled more than two-fifths of the manufacturing capital of the country and had affected about four-fifths of important American industries.[7]

the concentration of income

Accompanying this concentration of industry was an equally striking concentration of income in the hands of a small percentage of the population. Despite the fact that no accurate statistics for the early part of the period exist, it seems reasonably certain that the degree of concentration increased substantially between 1870 and 1929. By 1929, just 5 percent of the population received 34 percent of personal, disposable income in the United States.[8] The degree of concentration had probably reached this extreme as early as 1913. By the end of the 1920s, the highest one-fifth of "families and unattached individuals" were receiving in excess of 50 percent of all personal income.[9]

the reemergence of the classical liberal ideology

With this immense concentration of economic power in the hands of a small number of giant firms and a small percentage of the population, it would seem that the classical liberal ideology of capitalism would have been abandoned. The economic creed of classical

7 Joe S. Bain, "Industrial Concentration and Anti-Trust Policy," in Harold F. Williamson, ed., *Growth of the American Economy* (2d ed.; Englewood Cliffs, N.J.: Prentice-Hall, 1951), p. 619.

8 U.S. Department of Commerce, *Historical Statistics of the United States* (Washington, D.C.: U.S. Government Printing Office, 1961), p. 167.

9 Ibid., the data for 1913 do not give a figure for the income going to the top 5 percent. The amount going to the top 1 percent, however, was 14.98 percent in 1913 and 14.94 percent in 1928.

liberalism, as developed by Adam Smith and refined by such well-known classical economists as David Ricardo, Nassau Senior, and J. B. Say, was based on an analysis of an economy composed of many small enterprises. In such an economy, no individual enterprise could exercise a significant influence on the market price or on the total amount sold in the market. The actions of any firm were dictated to it by consumer tastes as registered in the marketplace and by the competition of innumerable other small firms, each vying for the consumers' dollars.

As wide as the gulf between classical economic theory and late nineteenth-century economic reality seems to have been, the economic creed of classical liberalism did not fall by the wayside in this later period. Rather, it was combined with Benthamite utilitarianism (which was already implicit in Adam Smith's normative model of the invisible hand) and refurbished within an elaborate and esoteric framework of algebra and calculus. This resurgence of the classical liberal economic creed was accomplished by a new school of economic thinkers known as *neoclassical* economists.

the neoclassical theory of utility and consumption

During the early 1870s, at precisely the time the drive toward the economic concentration of corporate capitalism was taking place, three very famous economics texts were published. William Stanley Jevons's *The Theory of Political Economy*[10] and Karl Menger's *Grundsätze der Volkswirtschaftslehre*[11] both appeared in 1871, and three years later, Léon Walras's *Eléments d'économie politique pure* was published.[12] Although there were many differences between the analyses of these men, the similarities in both approach and content of these books were striking.

Their theories pictured an economy made up of large numbers of small producers and consumers, each having insufficient power to influence the market significantly. The business firms hired or bought factors of production; they utilized the factors in the production process in such a way that their profits were maximized. Prices of the final products and factors of production were taken as given and

10 William Stanley Jevons, *The Theory of Political Economy* (1st ed.; London: Macmillan, 1871).

11 Karl Menger, *Grundsätze der Volkswirtschaftslehre* (Vienna: Braumuller, 1871), translated as *Principles of Economics* (New York: Free Press, 1950).

12 Léon Walras, *Eléments d'économie politique pure* (Lausanne: Corbaz et Cie, 1874); translated as *Elements of Pure Economics* (Homewood, Ill.: Irwin, 1954).

beyond their control. The firms could control only the productive process chosen and the amount produced.

Households likewise sold their land and capital, as well as their labor, at prices determined in the market and used the receipts (their incomes) to buy goods and services. Consumers apportioned their income among the various commodities they wished to purchase in a way that maximized the utility they received from these commodities.

Commodities were the ultimate source of pleasure or utility, and the utility they yielded was assumed to be quantifiable. Jevons wrote: "A unit of pleasure or pain is difficult even to conceive; but it is the amount of these feelings which is continually prompting us to buying and selling, borrowing and lending, laboring and resting, producing and consuming; *and it is from the quantitative effects of the feelings that we must estimate their comparative amounts.*"[13]

Walras was less ambiguous in arguing that utility was quantifiable: "I shall, therefore, assume the existence of a standard measure of intensity of wants or intensive utility, which is applicable not only to similar units of the same kind of wealth but also to different units of various kinds of wealth."[14]

These economists, having presumably quantifiable magnitudes with which to work, next set up general mathematical formulas purporting to show a functional relationship between the utility a consumer received and the amounts of the various commodities he consumed. The problem then was to show how the consumer could get the maximum utility, given his income and the commodity prices prevailing in the market.

Consumers maximized utility when the increase in utility derived from the last unit consumed, expressed as a ratio over the price of that commodity, was an equal proportion for all other commodities. In other words, the last dollar spent on a commodity should yield the same increase in the utility derived by the consumer as the last dollar spent on any other commodity. Jevons explained the same thing in a different way, stating that the consumer maximized utility because he "procures such quantities of commodities that the final degrees of utility of any pair of commodities are inversely as the ratios of exchange [prices] of the commodities."[15]

Suppose that their was a free market in which consumers could freely exchange their incomes for commodities. They would be led by their self-interest to maximize utility. Therefore, it was concluded that consumers distributed their income among the purchases of commodities in such a way that the welfare of all

13 Jevons, op. cit., p. 11.

14 Walras, op. cit., p. 117.

15 Jevons, op. cit., p. 139.

would be maximized, given the existing distribution of wealth and income.

the neoclassical theory of production

In neoclassical production theory, the analysis of the business firm was perfectly symmetrical to the analysis of consumer behavior. In order to maximize profits, the firm would operate at its highest efficiency and hence produce at the lowest possible cost. It purchased factors of production (such as labor) up to the point where the amount added to production by the last unit of each factor of production, expressed as a ratio over the price of the factor, was an equal proportion for all factors. The last dollar spent on each factor should yield the same increase in production from all factors. In a free market, firms would always attempt to maximize efficiency in order to maximize profits. Therefore this condition would always hold. Thus, the factors of production would all be used in such a way that no possible reorganization of production (given the existing technology) could result in a more efficient use of the factors of production.

Neoclassical economists also believed that if an economy were characterized by a free market with many small competitive firms, then each commodity would be produced in such quantities and with such methods that it would be impossible to shift resources from the production of one commodity to the production of a different commodity without diminishing the total value of what was produced in the market economy.

laissez faire

Thus, the neoclassical economists gave a very elaborate and esoteric analytical defense of Adam Smith's notion of the invisible hand of market competition and the economic policy of laissez faire. They showed that in a competitive market economy made up of innumerable small producers and consumers, the market would guide consumers in such a way that they would end up with an optimal mix of commodities, *given their original income and wealth.* Factors of production would be used in the most efficient way possible. Moreover, commodities would be produced in amounts that would maximize the value of society's production. This optimal result depended, however, on a minimum of interference by government in the processes of the free market.

They recognized that this result was optimal only if one accepted the existing distribution of income. Some (particularly the American economist John Bates Clark) tried to defend the distribution of income that obtained in a free-market economy. They argued that the principles of profit maximization would lead to a situation in which each category of productive factors would be paid an amount equal to the value of its marginal contribution to the productive process. This seemed to them to be a model of distributive justice, with each unit of the productive factors being paid an amount equal to what it produced. Critics were quick to point out, however, that units of productive factors were not people (at least as far as land, natural resources, and capital were concerned). In order for such a system to be fair, these critics insisted, an equitable distribution of ownership of the factors of production would be necessary.

Nevertheless, the neoclassical economists did succeed in erecting an impressive intellectual defense of the classical liberal policy of laissez faire. But they did it by creating a giant chasm between economic theory and economic reality. From the 1870s until today, many economists in the neoclassical tradition have abandoned any real concern with the existing economic institutions and problems. Instead, many of them have retired to the rarefied stratosphere of mathematical model-building, constructing endless variations on esoteric trivia.

subsequent modifications of neoclassical theory

Some economists in the second and third generations of neoclassical analysis recognized the need to make the theory more realistic. The economic system was *not* characterized by "perfect competition"; it had flaws. The principal admitted weaknesses were as follows: (1) Some buyers and sellers *were* large enough to affect prices, and, moreover, the economies of large-scale production seemed to render this inevitable. (2) Some commodities should be "consumed socially," and their production and sale might never be profitable in a laissez faire capitalist economy, even though they might be deemed highly desirable by most citizens (e.g., roads, schools, armies). (3) The costs to the producer of a commodity (such as automobiles) might differ significantly from the social costs (such as smog) of producing that commodity. In such a case, it was possible that for society as a whole, the costs of production might exceed the benefits of production for the commodity, even though the producer still profited from making and selling it. For example, consider the poisoning of the water and air by producers making profits but doing little or nothing about this evil, even though its side effects could endanger human life itself. (4) An unrestrained free-market capitalist system appeared to be quite unstable, being subject to recurring depressions that incurred enormous social waste.

It was generally agreed that such flaws did exist and did disrupt the otherwise-beneficial workings of the capitalist system, but they could only be corrected by some amount of government intervention into the market system. Government antitrust actions, it was argued, could force giant firms to act as if they were competitive, and something called "workable competition" could be achieved. Roads, schools, armies, and other socially consumed commodities could be provided by the government. Extensive systems of special taxes and subsidies could be used to equate private and social costs where they differed. Finally (especially after the 1930s), it was believed that through the wise use of fiscal and monetary policy, the government could eliminate the instability of the system. (This last point will be discussed in more detail in Chapter 10.)

The flaws were thus seen as minor and ephemeral. An enlightened government could correct them and free the invisible hand once again to create the best of all possible worlds. There did develop, however, an inability to agree on the extent and significance of the flaws. Those who believe them to be fairly widespread and quite significant have, during the course of the twentieth century, become known as *liberals.* They have sometimes advocated fairly extensive government intervention in the economic system, but most have continued to use neoclassical economic theory as an ideology to defend the private-ownership, capitalist market economic system.

Economists who see the flaws as minor and unimportant continue to advocate a minimum of government intervention in the market economy. Despite the fact that the laissez faire policies advocated by these economists have been much closer to those advocated by the nineteenth-century classical liberals, they have become known in the twentieth century as *conservatives.* Both liberals and conservatives, as we have described them here, have used neoclassical economic theory to justify the capitalist system.

laissez faire and the social darwinists

Before leaving the topic of late nineteenth- and early twentieth-century advocates of laissez faire capitalism, a brief discussion of *social Darwinism* is necessary. Social Darwinists believed the government should allow capitalists to compete freely in the marketplace with a minimum of government restrictions and, in general, favored as little government intervention as possible in all spheres of life. Therefore, many people have imagined their defense of laissez faire capitalism to be similar to that of the neoclassical economists. This is not so. Their policy recommendations were based on a substantially different theoretical framework.

The social Darwinists took Darwin's theory of evolution and extended it to a theory of social evolution (in a manner that Darwin himself strongly disapproved, it may be added). Competition, they believed, was a teleological process in which each succeeding generation was superior to the preceding generation. This upward progress was made possible because those least fit to survive did not succeed in maintaining themselves and procreating. Greater ability to survive was equated with a biological as well as a moral superiority.

Herbert Spencer (1820–1903), the father of social Darwinism, based his evolutionary theory as well as his moral theory on what he called the *law of conduct and consequence.* He believed the survival of the human species could be assured only if society distributed its benefits in proportion to a person's merit, which was measured by his power to sustain himself. Each person ought to reap the benefits or suffer the evil results of his own actions. Thus, the persons most adapted to their environment would prosper, and those least adapted would be weeded out—provided that the laws of conduct and consequence were observed. If the government, wishing to mitigate the inequalities of wealth and income in society, took "from him who . . . [had] prospered to give to him who . . . [had] not, it [violated] its duty towards the one to do more than its duty towards the other."[16] This type of action slowed social progress and could, if carried to excess, destroy the human species. Survival and progress could be assured only if the weak were weeded out and destroyed by the impersonal forces of social evolution.

In Spencer's opinion, "the poverty of the incapable, the distresses that come upon the imprudent, the starvation of the idle, and those shoulderings aside of the weak by the strong . . . are the decrees of a large, far-seeing benevolence."[17] Spencer categorically opposed any action by the government that interfered with trade, commerce, production, or the distribution of wealth or income. He rejected welfare payments of any kind, attempts to decrease the economic insecurity of workers, and government's provision of schools, parks, or libraries as detrimental to human progress. His laissez faire was

16 Quoted in Sidney Fine, *Laissez Faire and the General Welfare State* (Ann Arbor, Mich.: University of Michigan Press, 1964), p. 38.

17 Ibid.

thus much more extreme than that of the classical economists or most of the conservative neoclassical economists.

Social Darwinists accepted the large monopolistic and oligopolistic industries as the beneficent result of evolution. Neoclassical economists, if they did not simply define away or ignore the concentrations of economic power, believed that government should attempt to create a more competitive and atomistic market situation. Thus, in this very important respect, the two theories were quite antagonistic.

laissez faire and the ideology of businessmen

Most businessmen, however, were not very concerned with intellectual consistency. They feared radical and socialist reformers who wanted to use the government as a means of achieving greater equality; and they welcomed any theory that concluded that the government should not intervene in the economic process. Even though they themselves used the government extensively to promote their own interests (through special tariffs, tax concessions, land grants, and a host of other special privileges), they relied on laissez faire arguments when threatened with any social reform that might erode their status, influence, wealth, or income. Thus, in the ordinary businessman's ideology of the late nineteenth and early twentieth centuries, there was a general attempt to combine neoclassical economics and social Darwinism.

In this ideology, the accumulation of wealth was considered de facto proof of evolutionary superiority, whereas poverty was believed to be evidence of evolutionary inferiority. Success, asserted writer Benjamin Woods, was "nothing more or less than doing thoroughly what others did indifferently." Andrew Carnegie equated success with "honest work, ability and concentration"; another businessman argued that "wealth has always been the natural sequence to industry, temperance, and perseverance, and it will always so continue." At the same time, S. C. T. Dodd, solicitor for Standard Oil, maintained that poverty existed "because nature or the devil has made some men weak and imbecile and others lazy and worthless, and neither man nor God can do much for one who will do nothing for himself."[18]

The beneficial results of competition in neoclassical economic theory seemed to reinforce reliance on the "survival of the fittest" in the "struggle for survival." "Competition in economics," asserted

[18] All quotations in this paragraph are cited in Fine, op. cit., p. 98.

Richard R. Bowker, "is the same as the law of . . . 'natural selection' in nature."[19]

Although some businessmen and their spokesmen were trying to perpetuate the laissez faire conclusions of the classical liberal ideology of capitalism, many defenders of the capitalist system believed that in the new age of mass production (with gigantic concentrations of wealth and power in the hands of so few corporations and capitalists), the older, individualistic, laissez faire ideology was no longer appropriate. The late nineteenth century witnessed a rebirth of the older paternalistic ethic. In Chapter 8, we will examine a new ideology of capitalism that was based, in many essential respects, on a new version of the Christian corporate ethic.

summary

In the late nineteenth century, capitalism was characterized by the growth of giant corporations. Control of most of the important industries became more and more concentrated. Accompanying this concentration of industry was an equally striking concentration of income in the hands of a small percentage of the population.

In view of these facts, it would seem that the classical liberal ideology (which was based on an analysis of an economy based on many small, relatively powerless enterprises) would have to be abandoned. The gulf that separated the theory from reality had widened into a giant chasm. But the idea that the market economy channeled acquisitive profit-seeking into socially benevolent practices was simply too elegant an apologia for unrestrained profit-making. So the classical liberal ideology of capitalism was even more assiduously disseminated in a new school of neoclassical economics.

An elaborate deductive theory permitted the neoclassical economists to defend the classical policy prescription of laissez faire. Conservative neoclassical economists assigned to the government only those tasks that would directly or indirectly promote business profits. Liberal neoclassical economists also believed the government should enter a limited number of other areas in which the operation of the free market did not maximize the social welfare. Whether in the hands of the conservative or the liberal faction, neoclassical economics remained essentially an ideological defense for the status quo.

Finally, social Darwinist ideology and the ideology of most businessmen defended many of the neoclassical economists' con-

[19] Ibid., p. 100.

clusions. They did so, however, on entirely different grounds. They accepted the fact that corporate power, personal wealth, and personal income were highly concentrated. This, they believed, was evidence of the evolutionary superiority of the wealthy and, as such, was socially beneficial.

chapter 8
the consolidation of monopoly power and the new christian corporate ethic

The process of industrialization in the United States after the Civil War involved, in its initial stages, a competition among industrial and financial capitalists that was unique in its ferocity. From 1860 until the early 1880s, the strongest and shrewdest businessmen built great empires with the fruits of economic conquest. The great improvements in transportation that occurred in the period, the rise of standardization in parts and finished products, and the increased efficiency in large-scale mass production created the possibility of nationwide markets. The stakes in the economic struggle were very large, and the participants neither asked for nor received quarter.

competition as industrial warfare

Examples of the industrial warfare have filled many books.[1] In the oil industry, for example, John D. Rockefeller and Henry M. Flagler shipped so much oil that they were able to demand large concessions from the railroads. With this cost advantage, they could undersell competitors. Their company (which was incorporated in 1870 under the name of Standard Oil Company of Ohio) was able to force many

[1] See, for example, Matthew Josephson, *The Robber Barons* (New York: Harcourt Brace Jovanovich, Harvest Books, 1962), for a fascinating account of the exploits of the capitalists of this era.

competitors to the wall and to achieve regional monopolies, at which point the price could be substantially increased without fear of competition. After securing their large rebates on transport costs, Standard Oil's share in the petroleum industry quickly increased from 10 to 20 percent. But they did not stop there. They next succeeded in forcing the railroads to give them rebates on their *competitor's* shipments as well as "all data relating to shipper, buyer, product, price and terms of payment," a scheme that "provided Rockefeller and his associates with rebates on all their own shipments, rebates on all shipments by their competitors, and in addition a complete spy system on their competitors."[2] With this power, Rockefeller was able to smash most of his competitors. By 1879, only nine years after incorporation, Standard Oil controlled between 90 and 95 percent of the nation's output of refined petroleum. A sympathetic biographer of Rockefeller has written: "Of all the devices for the extinction of competition, this was the cruelest and most deadly yet conceived by any group of American industrialists."[3]

Competition among the railroad magnates was particularly intense. Rate wars were common, forcing weaker competitors out of business and giving stronger competitors monopoly powers over large regions. The battles sometimes got so brutal that locomotives were crashed into each other and track was destroyed. The railroads also extorted money from towns along proposed railroad lines. A member of the California Constitutional Convention of 1878 described the technique:

> They start out their railroad track and survey their line near a thriving village. They go to the most prominent citizens of that village and say, 'If you will give us so many thousand dollars we will run through here; if you do not we will run by.' And in every instance where the subsidy was not granted this course was taken and the effect was just as they said, to kill off the little town.[4]

According to that same report, the railroad "blackmailed Los Angeles County for $230,000 as a condition of doing that which the law compelled them to do." The railroads also manipulated connections with politicians to get government handouts of public lands. It is estimated that these giveaways amounted to 158,293,000 acres—more land than is contained in some whole countries.[5] The

2 Dudley Dillard, *Economic Development of the North Atlantic Community* (Englewood Cliffs, N.J.: Prentice-Hall, 1967), p. 410.

3 Allan Nevins, *John D. Rockefeller, The Heroic Age of American Enterprise,* vol. 1 (New York: Scribner's, 1940), p. 325.

4 Quoted in Josephson, op. cit., pp. 84–85.

5 Ibid., p. 79.

railroads were certainly not in favor of a laissez faire policy in practice.

The great entrepreneurs of that age were definitely not men of estimable social conscience. Many founded their fortunes on the Civil War. When shortages of supplies became desperate, they received high prices for selling to the army "shoddy blankets, so many doctored horses and useless rifles, [and] . . . stores of sickening beef."[6] In order to eliminate their competitors, they did not hesitate to use hired thugs, kidnappings, and dynamiting. Likewise, they stopped at nothing as they mulcted the public of millions of dollars through stock frauds, schemes, and swindles. Some of these actions were legal and some were not, but the dominant mood of these capitalist entrepreneurs was expressed by Cornelius Vanderbilt, who, when cautioned about the questionable legality of a desired course of action, exclaimed, "What do I care about the law? Hain't I got the power?"[7] Much the same idea was expressed by William Vanderbilt during a public outcry against one of his policy decisions: "The public be damned. I am working for my stockholders."[8]

business collusion and government regulation

After a few years of this type of competition, however, most of the remaining business firms were battle-tested giants. Continuing such competition would have been ruinous for all. So, whereas competition was the road to large profits before 1880, after that date, it became obvious that cooperative collusion would be more beneficial for the remaining firms. In that way, they could exercise monopolistic power for their mutual benefit. Thus, pools, trusts, and mergers (described in Chapter 7) were the consequence of the earlier competition. Increasingly, as the turn of the century neared, the neoclassical vision of many small competing firms diverged from the reality of massive corporations acting cooperatively to maximize their joint profits.

With the rise of big corporations, there was a parallel growth of grass-roots popular opposition to these companies and their blatant disregard for the public welfare. This popular antagonism became so

[6] Ibid., p. 67.

[7] Ibid., p. 72.

[8] Ibid.

widespread and intense that in the presidential campaign of 1888, both the Democrats and the Republicans advocated federal laws to curb the abuses of big corporations.

After the 1888 election, both parties became extremely reluctant to take any such action. Many of the most important Republicans controlled the very corporations they had promised to curb, and the Democrats were but slightly less involved with big business. Only when public pressure reached incredible heights did Congress respond, in December 1889, by passing the Sherman Antitrust Act. The act, an obvious concession to an aroused public opinion, passed both houses of Congress with only a single dissenting vote. But the law was so weak and vaguely worded that it appeared to be designed to insure that it would be ineffective. Another proposal that recommended meaningful punishment of firms who violated the law was overwhelmingly defeated.

The law proscribed "every contract, combination in the form of a trust or otherwise, or conspiracy, in restraint of trade or commerce among the several states or with foreign nations. . . ." It also declared a person guilty of a misdemeanor if he attempted "to monopolize, or combine or conspire with any other person . . . to monopolize any part of the trade or commerce among the several states, or with foreign nations. . . ."

The primary effect of the Sherman Act over the next few decades was to weaken labor unions. What had begun as a concession to the public's hatred of big business' abuses became an antilabor law as the courts ruled that many union strikes constituted constraints of trade.

While President McKinley was in office, there were only five cases initiated under the Sherman Act, despite the fact that there were 146 major industrial combinations formed between the years 1899 and 1901 alone. One of these was the massive United States Steel Corporation, which in 1901 controlled or acquired 785 plants worth a whopping $1,370,000,000.

Staggeringly high profits, graft, corruption, and discriminatory practices on the part of the nation's railroads led to the establishment of the first federal government regulatory agency. The Interstate Commerce Act of 1887 established the Interstate Commerce Commission (ICC), which was designed to regulate the railroads in order to protect the public interest.

Competition among the railroads had been so destructive that the railroads themselves were the leading advocates of extended federal regulation. A few years after the passage of the Interstate Commerce Act, U.S. Attorney General Olney wrote a letter to a railroad president that read, in part: "The Commission [ICC] . . . is, or can be made, of great use to the railroads. It satisfies the popular clamor for a government supervision of railroads, at the same time that supervision is almost entirely nominal. Further, the older such a commission gets to be, the more inclined it will be found to take the business and railroad view of things. . . ."[9]

The attorney general's prediction has certainly been borne out by the facts. In the years since the establishment of the ICC, many other federal regulatory agencies have been established. The Federal Communications Commission (FCC), the Civil Aeronautics Board (CAB), and the Securities Exchange Commission (SEC) were among the federal agencies that joined the ICC as "protectors" of the public interest. Most serious students of government regulation would agree that "the outstanding political fact about the . . . regulatory commissions is that they have in general become promoters and protectors of the industries they have been established to regulate."[10]

Thus, in many oligopolistic industries, there was an inability to cooperate and to act collectively as a monopoly. For these industries, there is a considerable body of evidence indicating that they turned to the government and to federal regulatory agencies as a means of achieving this monopolistic coordination.[11] Regulatory agencies have generally performed this function very effectively.

The collusive behavior of the oligopolistic businesses seemed to go unnoticed by neoclassical economists. They continued to frame their analyses in terms of innumerable small, competing business firms. In their advocacy of laissez faire policies, they failed to see that it was primarily big business that supported active government intervention.

Neoclassical economists also continued to accept the classical economists' view that as long as free competition prevails, the economy will tend toward a full utilization of its productive capacity and full employment will more or less continuously prevail. During the last half of the nineteenth century, however, economic depressions became more frequent and more severe. During the first half of the nineteenth century, the United States had had two economic crises (in 1819 and 1837), and England had had four (in 1815, 1825, 1836, and 1847). During the last half of the century, the number increased to five in the United States (in 1854, 1857, 1873, 1884, and 1893), and six in England (in 1857, 1866, 1873, 1882, 1890 and 1900). Thus, the neoclassical economic ideology was as poor a

9 Quoted in Grant McConnell, "Self-Regulation, The Politics of Business," in D. Mermelstein, ed., *Economics: Mainstream Readings and Radical Critiques* (New York: Random House, 1970), p. 197.

10 Ibid., p. 199.

11 The most thoroughly documented defense of this assertion can be found in Gabriel Kolko, *The Triumph of Conservatism* (New York: Free Press, 1963).

reflection of economic performance as it was of industrial concentration.

a new christian corporate ethic

The distance separating the neoclassical liberal ideology of capitalism and economic reality impressed itself on the minds of many academicians and businessmen. The result was a new ideology for the new age of corporate capitalism. Just as the new industrial and financial entrepreneurs came to resemble the feudal robber barons, so the new ideology resembled the feudal version of the Christian corporate ethic. It emphasized the natural superiority of a small elite (the new industrial and financial magnates) and the paternalistic functions of that elite in caring for the masses.

The new ideology reflected the fact that many of the wealthy capitalists of the era were becoming something of folk heroes among the general public. The last two decades of the nineteenth century and the first three of the twentieth were an age during which the businessman became the most admired social type. Their success was viewed as de facto proof that they possessed virtues superior to those of the ordinary man. This version of success was the theme of the biographies of William Makepeace Thackeray and the novels of Horatio Alger. These men and other writers created a cult of success that viewed the increase of industrial concentration as proof of a Darwinian superiority of the industrialists, glorified the self-made man, and kept the Horatio Alger myth of rags to riches constantly in the public mind.

This veneration of businessmen, added to the strong rejection of destructive competition by both the businessmen and the general public, led to a new conservative version of the Christian corporate ethic, which resembled the philosophy of the Tory radicals of the late eighteenth and early nineteenth centuries. The unfortunate plight of the poor received prominent mention in the new writings. This problem as well as that of economic instability could best be solved, according to the new ideology, by encouraging cooperation among the leaders of the giant corporations. Competition was viewed as antisocial. Through cooperation, business cycles could be eliminated and the plight of the poor could be improved.

This new version of the Christian corporate ethic received the support of Pope Leo XIII (1810–1903). Between 1878 and 1901, the pope sought to analyze the problems of corporate capitalism and to suggest remedies in a series of encyclicals. In *Rerum novarum* (1891), he argued that "a remedy must be found . . . for the misery and wretchedness which press so heavily at this moment on the large majority of the very poor." He continued with a condemnation of unrestrained laissez faire competition.

> Working men have been given over, isolated and defenseless, to the callousness of employers and the greed of unrestrained competition. The evil has been increased by rapacious usury . . . still practiced by avaricious and grasping men. And to this must be added the custom of working by contract, and the concentration of so many branches of trade in the hands of a few individuals, so that a small number of very rich men have been able to lay upon the masses of the poor a yoke little better than slavery itself.[12]

This passage, which sounds so socialist in tone and content, was followed by a strong condemnation of socialism and a defense of private property. The pope hoped the problems could be corrected by rejection of competition and a return to the Christian virtues of love and brotherhood, with the leaders of business and industry leading the way to a new Christian paternalism within the context of a private property capitalist system.

THE GERMAN VERSION

The new paternalistic ideology was probably strongest in Germany, where classical liberalism had really never gained a good hold and where industrial concentration was most pronounced. A famous German economist expressed the very widely held view that

> the proper kind of cartelization creates more or less a system of justice and equity. . . . The directors of the cartels are educators who wish to bring about the triumph of wide interests of a branch of industry over the egoistic interests of the individual. . . . The cartel system is, like a co-operative or merchants' association, an important element in the education of commercial and technical officials who want to make money but who have also learned to put themselves in the service of general interests and to administer the property of others in a loyal and honorable fashion.[13]

Cartels were also widely justified as means of eliminating economic crises. A German court decision, one of several that formed the legal justification of the cartel system in that country, stated: "Indeed the formation of syndicates and cartels . . . has repeatedly been considered a device especially useful for the economy as a

12 Quoted in Daniel R. Fusfeld, *The Age of the Economist* (Glenview, Ill.: Scott, Foresman, 1966), p. 86.

13 Gustave Schmoller, quoted in Koppel S. Pinson, *Modern Germany: Its History and Civilization* (New York: Macmillan, 1954), p. 236.

whole, since they can prevent uneconomic overproduction and ensuing catastrophe."[14]

THE AMERICAN VERSION

In the United States, as was mentioned above, the new ideology thrived in an atmosphere that venerated the successful businessman and was extremely weary of destructive competition. The view of many American industrial and financial magnates was expressed by Andrew Carnegie (one of the most successful of the magnates):

> Not evil, but good, has come to the race from the accumulation of wealth by those who have the ability and energy that produce it. . . . We have the true antidote for the temporary unequal distribution of wealth, the reconciliation of the rich and the poor—a reign of harmony—another ideal, differing, indeed, from that of the Communist in requiring only further evolution of existing conditions, not the total overthrow of our civilization. . . . Under its sway we shall have an ideal state, in which the surplus wealth of the few will become in the best sense, the property of the many, because administered for the common good, this wealth passing through the hands of the few can be made a more potent force for the elevation of our race than if it were distributed in sums to the people themselves.[15]

Carnegie argued, and many businessmen and their spokesmen agreed, that the millionaire would be "a trustee for the poor, entrusted for a season with a great part of the increased wealth of the community, but administering it for the community far better than it could or would have done for itself."[16]

The Right Reverend William Lawrence gave the new elitist view the sanction of religion. "In the long run, it is only to the man of morality that wealth comes. . . . Godliness is in league with riches."[17] And railroad President George F. Baer had the same idea in mind when he tried to assure railroad workers that "the rights and the interests of the laboring man will be protected and cared for, not by the labor agitators, but by the Christian men to whom God in his infinite wisdom, has given control of the property interests of the country."[18]

14 Quoted in Dillard, op. cit., p. 396.

15 Andrew Carnegie, "Wealth," in Gail Kennedy, ed., *Democracy and the Gospel of Wealth* (Lexington, Mass.: Raytheon/Heath, 1949), pp. 3, 5, and 6.

16 Cited in Kennedy, op. cit., p. xii.

17 Ibid.

18 Ibid.

simon patten's economic basis for the new ethic

Perhaps the most influential academic spokesman for the new corporate ideology was Dr. Simon N. Patten, professor of economics at the University of Pennsylvania from 1888 to 1917 and one of the founders of the American Economic Association.[19] In keeping with the paternalistic element of the new ideology, Patten denounced the poverty and economic exploitation of his era. The following passage could almost have been written by a Marxist of that era:

> There have flowed then, side by side, two streams of life, one bearing the working poor, who perpetuate themselves through qualities generated by the stress and mutual dependence of the primitive world, and the other bearing aristocracies, who dominate by means of the laws and traditions giving them control of the social surplus.[20]

in the same vein, fifteen years later, he wrote that

> The glow of Fifth Avenue is but the reflection of a distant hell into which unwilling victims are cast. Some resource is misused, some town degraded, to create the flow of funds on which our magnates thrive. From Pennsylvania, rich in resources, trains go loaded and come back empty. For the better half no return is made except in literary tomes designed to convince the recipients that exploitation is not robbery. . . . But Nature revolts! Never does the rising sun see children yanked from bed to increase the great Strauss dividends, nor the veteran cripples of the steel mill tramping in their beggar garb, but that it shrivels, reddens, and would strike but for the sight of happier regions beyond.[21]

This poverty and exploitation were, in Patten's opinion, the last vestiges of an earlier age characterized by scarcity. In the economy of scarcity, capitalists aggressively competed with each other, with the result that laborers as well as the general public suffered. The fierce competition of the robber barons, however, had marked a watershed in history. The merger movement that followed this competition was the beginning of a new era, an era of plenty rather

19 For a more complete account of Patten's ideas see E. K. Hunt, "Simon N. Patten's Contribution to Economics," *Journal of Economic Issues* (December 1970), pp. 38–55.

20 Simon Nelson Patten, *The New Basis of Civilization* (New York: Macmillan, 1907), p. 39.

21 Simon Nelson Patten, *Mud Hollow* (Philadelphia: Dorrance, 1922), p. 226.

than of scarcity. Capitalists were becoming socialized. They were putting the public welfare ahead of their pursuit of profits, and in doing this, they eschewed competition, recognizing that the public welfare could be best promoted by cooperation.

Evidence that the conditions of economic prosperity at the turn of the century were socializing capitalists could be gotten from the fact that "hospitals . . . [were] established, schools . . . [were] made free, colleges . . . [were] endowed, museums, libraries, and art galleries . . . [received] liberal support, church funds . . . [grew] and missions . . . [were] formed at home and abroad."[22] On almost every policy issue of his day, Patten took a strongly proindustrial capitalist position. He viewed the late nineteenth-century captains of industry as a paternally beneficent elite:

> The growth of large-scale capitalism has resulted in the elimination of the unsocial capitalist and the increasing control of each industry by the socialized groups. . . . At bottom altruistic sentiment is the feeling of a capitalist expressing itself in sympathy for the laborer. This desire of upper class men to improve the conditions of lower classes is a radically different phenomenon from the pressure exerted by the lower classes for their own betterment. The lower class movement stands for the control of the state by themselves in their own interests. The upper class movement directs itself against the bad environmental conditions preventing the expression of character.[23]

He believed that competition should be discouraged by taxing competitive firms and exempting trusts and monopolies from these taxes. This would benefit all society by eliminating the extensive waste created by competition. In *The Stability of Prices,* he argued that competition was largely responsible for the economic instability of the late nineteenth century. When the movement toward trusts and monopolies had been completed, production would be controlled and planned in such a way that this instability would be eliminated.

Patten's paternalistic ideology was, like the liberal ideology of capitalism, ultimately a plea for a minimum of government interference with the actions of businessmen. The government was to interfere in the economy only by encouraging trusts and monopolies and discouraging competition. In Patten's scheme, all important social and economic reforms were to be carried out voluntarily by the socialized capitalists in a system of cooperative corporate collectivism.

22 Simon Nelson Patten, *The Theory of Prosperity* (New York: Macmillan, 1902), p. 170.

23 Simon Nelson Patten, "The Reconstruction of Economic Theory," reprinted in Simon Nelson Patten, *Essays in Economic Theory,* ed. Rexford Guy Tugwell (New York: Knopf, 1924), p. 292.

the new paternalism and the new deal[24]

Patten's version of the new ideology of corporate capitalism was to be very important historically. When the Great Depression of the 1930s struck, two of Patten's students and devotees, Rexford Guy Tugwell and Frances Perkins, had influential positions as members of Roosevelt's original cabinet. Tugwell had asserted that Patten's views "were the greatest single influence on my thought. Neither Veblen nor Dewey found their orientation to the future as completely and instinctively as did Patten. The magnificence of his conceptions and the basic rightness of his vision become clearer as time passes. I am eternally grateful to him."[25] Miss Perkins believed her former teacher to be "one of the greatest men America has ever produced."[26]

Through these two former students, Patten exerted a considerable influence on the economic policies of the early phase of the New Deal. His ideas helped to create the intellectual basis of the National Industrial Recovery Act of 1933 (NIRA).[27] Patten was not, of course, the only source of these ideas. During World War I, the War Industries Board had generated enthusiasm for corporate collectivism. Throughout the 1920s, trade associations prospered, and the doctrine of business self-government gained many adherents in the busines world. In 1922, Franklin Roosevelt had been president of one such association: the American Construction Council. However, Patten's teachings were unquestionably influential. His two protégés, Tugwell and Perkins, were both instrumental in the actual framing of the NIRA.

The National Industrial Recovery Act proclaimed the intent of Congress "to promote the organization of industry for the purpose of cooperative action among trade groups."[28] The bill contained sections providing for codes of fair competition that permitted and even encouraged cooperative price-fixing and market-sharing and for virtually complete exemption from antitrust laws. Section 7A was designed to promote labor organization but was so diluted that very

24 For a more complete discussion of the material covered in this section, see E. K. Hunt, "A Neglected Aspect of the Economic Ideology of the Early New Deal," *Review of Social Economy* (September 1971), pp. 180–192.

25 Quoted in Allan G. Gruchy, *Modern Economic Thought: The American Contribution* (New York: Augustus M. Kelley, 1967), p. 408.

26 Quoted in Arthur M. Schlesinger, Jr., *The Coming of the New Deal* (Boston: Houghton Mifflin, 1965), p. 229.

27 Schlesinger, op. cit., p. 98.

28 Quoted in ibid., pp. 98–99.

often it promoted the formation of company unions. "If it [the NIRA] worked, Tugwell thought, each industry would end with a government of its own under which it could promote its fundamental purpose ('production rather than competition'). NRA could have been administered, Tugwell later wrote, so that a 'great collectivism' would have channeled American energy into a disciplined national effort to establish a secure basis for well-being."[29]

In explaining the bill to the National Association of Manufacturers, General Hugh S. Johnson, the first head of the National Recovery Administration (NRA) declared that "NRA is exactly what industry organized in trade associations makes it." He further asserted that before the NRA, the trade associations had about as much effectiveness as an "Old Ladies' Knitting Society; now I am talking to a cluster of formerly emasculated trade associations about a law which proposes for the first time to give them power."[30]

Most of the economic literature which appeared in 1934 recognized that the early New Deal reforms had not significantly extended government control over business. On the contrary, it had given voluntary trade associations the support of the government in forcing the controls of the trade associations on all industry.[31]

This experience in business self-government proved to be disastrous. The distinguished historian Arthur M. Schlesinger, Jr., has assessed the success of this phase of the early New Deal. With Schlesinger, we concur:

> And the result of business self-government? Restriction on production, chiseling of labor and of 7A, squeezing out of small business, savage personal criticism of the President, and the general tendency to trample down every one in the rush for profits. Experience was teaching Roosevelt what instinct and doctrine has taught Jefferson and Jackson; that, to reform capitalism you must fight the capitalists tooth and nail.[32]

The early New Deal philosophy underlying the NIRA was very quickly abandoned, and the NIRA was declared unconstitutional. The new paternalistic ideology of capitalism, however, was to receive more elaborate statements after World War II. (These

29 Ibid., p. 108.

30 General Hugh S. Johnson, quoted in ibid., p. 110.

31 See Leo Rogin, "The New Deal: A Survey of Literature," *Quarterly Journal of Economics* (May 1935), pp. 338, 346, and 349–355. Typical of the comments of supporters of the early New Deal is this quotation from Tilly: "Here *industry* is setting up a legal and enforceable Golden Rule." Ibid., p. 351.

32 Arthur M. Schlesinger, Jr., "The Broad Accomplishments of the New Deal," in Edwin C. Rozwenc, ed., *The New Deal: Revolution or Evolution* (Lexington, Mass.: Raytheon/Heath, 1959), pp. 30–31.

statements and the later New Deal policies will be discussed in subsequent chapters.)

summary

The industrial warfare of the late nineteenth century led to an era of mergers and collusion among the giant corporations. Through collusion, the few corporations that controlled an industry could act effectively as monopolists and maximize their joint profits. Where collusion was difficult, the corporations relied heavily on government regulatory agencies to help enforce mutual cooperation.

Within this economic and political context, many ideologists of capitalism rejected classical liberalism because of its unrealistic assumptions. These thinkers created a new version of the Christian corporate ethic that pictured the new industrial and financial magnates as beneficent, paternalistic protectors of the public welfare.

This new ethic was to become particularly influential in the social and economic legislation of the early New Deal of the 1930s.

chapter 9
evolutionary socialism and imperialism

In the late nineteenth and early twentieth centuries, the socialist analysis of capitalism was profoundly affected by two developments: (1) the economic and political gains made by the working class and (2) the imperialistic carving-up of the economically less-developed areas of the world by the major capitalist powers.

the economic and political gains of the working class

During the last half of the nineteenth century, the real income of workers rose throughout the capitalist world. In England, the average real wage increased rapidly throughout the 1860s and early 1870s. By 1875, it was 40 percent higher that it had been in 1862. After ten years in which wages sagged, they again rose sharply between 1885 and 1900. By 1900, the average real wage was 33 percent higher than in 1875 and 84 percent higher than in 1850. Most of the gains in real wages are attributable to the advent of mass-production techniques which permitted prices of many commodities laborers consumed to be lowered. With the new methods of producing and labor's greater purchasing power, there was a fundamental change in patterns of consumption. Workingmen began to eat more meats, fruits, and sweets. Cafés, mass-produced shoes and clothing, furniture, newspapers, bicycles, and other new products came to be within the reach of many. Unquestionably, the average workingman's lot improved substantially during the period.

It should be mentioned, however, that averages can be misleading. Two late nineteenth-century social surveys revealed that about 40 percent of the working class in London and York still lived in abject poverty. The fact that this could be so after a half century of rapid increases in average real wages gives an indication of the truly pitiful conditions that must have existed in the early nineteenth century.

Similar gains were being made in western Europe and the United States during the period, and the economic gains were accompanied in most of the countries by political gains. Most of the industrialized capitalist countries had nearly complete male suffrage by the early twentieth century. Political parties were created that were devoted to furthering the cause of workingmen. Despite at times harsh efforts to repress them, the German Social Democratic party, most of whose leaders professed to be Marxists, polled 549,000 votes in 1884 and 763,000 votes in 1887; by 1890, they were the largest single party in the Reichstag, having polled 1,427,000 votes.

the fabian socialists

In England, despite the brilliant achievements of individual Marxists such as William Morris, the socialist movement was largely non-Marxist. The Fabian Society was the primary influence on English socialism, and they rejected Marx's analysis completely. In their economic analysis, the Fabians used orthodox neoclassical utility theory. Labor received, they believed, an amount equal to what it produced, and capitalists and landlords received the value of what was produced with their capital and land. The chief cause of injustice was not that labor's surplus value was appropriated by capitalists, but rather that all the income from ownership accrued to a tiny percentage of the population. The only way to achieve an equitable society would be to divide the income from ownership equally, and this could be done only through government ownership of the means of production.

On the issue of the nature and role of the government, the Fabians differed radically from Marx. For Marx, the government was an instrument of coercion controlled and used by the ruling class to perpetuate the privileges inherent in the capitalist system. The Fabians believed that in a parliamentary democracy based upon universal suffrage, the state was a neutral agency which could be freely used by the majority to reform the social and economic system. Because the working class was the majority in a capitalist economy, they were confident that, step by step, piecemeal reforms would strip away the privileges of the owning class and result in socialism achieved by peaceful evolution rather than violent revolution.

The Fabian Society gradually succeeded in gaining influence in the parliamentary Labour party. By 1918, the Labour party adopted a socialist program that reflected the Fabian Society's views and attitudes. By the 1920s, the Labour party had formed a government, and the cause of socialism via the voting booth seemed to many to be on the road to triumph.

The Fabians had never wanted to be a mass-membership society. A small, select group, they hoped to educate the middle class to accept socialism. They published innumerable tracts exposing the poverty and injustice they found in early twentieth-century England. Remedies for these evils would be forthcoming through paternalistic government actions and programs, they believed, once the government was made truly democratic and the people were made aware of these conditions.

However debatable their certainty that socialism could be achieved through education, it is undeniable that the Fabians offered an impressive group of teachers. Some of the most brilliant of the English intellectual elite were members of the society, including Sidney and Beatrice Webb, George Bernard Shaw, H. G. Wells, Sydney Olivier, and Graham Wallas. With such sponsorship, the Fabians' reformist, evolutionary socialism became eminently respectable. One could espouse socialism and still remain completely secure in one's comfortable middle-class niche in English capitalistic society.

the german revisionists

The German counterparts of the English Fabians were the revisionists. At the turn of the century, the Social Democratic party was nominally a Marxist party. A large segment of the membership, however, argued that the course of history had proven Marx wrong on many issues and that a "revision" of Marx's ideas was necessary to make them relevant to German economic and social life. The most famous of the revisionists was Eduard Bernstein, who presented a detailed critique of Marxist ideas in his best-known work, *Evolutionary Socialism,* which was published in 1899. Bernstein maintained that capitalism was not approaching any kind of crisis or collapse, and indeed that it had never been more viable. Marx was also wrong, Bernstein declared, in predicting the concentration of all industries in the hands of a few giant firms. He argued that enterprises of all sizes thrived and would continue to do so (despite the fact that corporate concentration and the cartel movement were more extreme in Germany than in any other capitalist country). Even if large trusts did dominate the economy, Bernstein insisted, there would be a "splitting up of shares," making petty capitalists of a very large percentage of the population, including many workers. He believed the economy had already gone far in this direction: "The number of members of the possessing classes is today not smaller but larger. The enormous increase of social wealth is not accompanied by a decreasing number of large capitalists, but by an increasing number of capitalists of all degrees."[1]

Thus, in continental Europe, as well as in England, the idea that a democratic government in a capitalist country could be used to effect a gradual and peaceful transition from capitalism to socialism received widespread support, and evolutionary socialism appeared to be displacing the revolutionary socialism of the Marxists. However, events of the late nineteenth and early twentieth centuries significantly weakened the solidarity of the evolutionary socialists, particularly the Fabians. This was the period during which European economic imperialism was most intensive. The nature and importance of and the appropriate socialist response to imperialism were issues that created a profound division of socialist opinion—and one that persists to this day.

european imperialism

India was one of the earliest and most dramatic cases of European imperialism. The East India Company had traded extensively in India for 150 years prior to the conquest of Bengal in 1757. During this period, India was relatively advanced economically. Her methods of production and her industrial and commercial organization could definitely be compared with those prevailing in western Europe. In fact, India had been manufacturing and exporting the finest muslins and luxurious fabrics since the time when most western Europeans were backward, primitive peoples.

But after the conquest, the East India Company became the ruling

1 Eduard Bernstein, *Evolutionary Socialism* (New York: Schocken Books, 1961 [first published in 1899]), p. xii.

power in much of India, and the trade of the previous 150 years turned to harsh exploitation. It has been estimated that between 1757 and 1815, the British took between £500 million and £1,000 million of wealth out of India.[2] The incredible magnitude of this sum can only be appreciated when compared with the £36 million that represented the total capital investment of all the joint-stock companies that were operating in India.[3]

The policy of the East India Company in the last decades of the eighteenth century and in the early nineteenth century reflected two objectives. First, in the short run, the myriad of greedy officials sought personal fortunes overnight: "These officials were absolute, irresponsible and rapacious, and they emptied the private hoards. Their only thought was to wring some hundreds of thousands of pounds out of the natives as quickly as possible, and hurry home to display their wealth. Enormous fortunes were thus rapidly accumulated at Calcutta, while thirty millions of human beings were reduced to the extremity of wretchedness."[4]

A British observer described this ruthless quest for wealth in similar terms: "No Mahratta raid ever devastated a countryside with the thoroughness with which both the Company [East India Company] and, above all, the Company's servants in their individual capacities, sucked dry the plain of Bengal. In fact, in their blind rage for enrichment they took more from the Bengali peasants than those peasants could furnish and live. And the peasants duly died."[5]

The second was a long-run goal: to discourage or eliminate Indian manufacturers and to make India dependent on British industries by forcing the Indians to concentrate on raw materials and export them to supply the textile looms and other British manufacturers. The policy was brutally and methodically—and successfully—executed.

> The total effect of this was that the British administration of India systematically destroyed all the fibres and foundations of Indian society. Its land and taxation policy ruined India's village economy and substituted for it the parasitic landowner and moneylender. Its commercial policy destroyed the Indian artisan and created the infamous slums of the Indian cities filled with millions of starving and diseased paupers. Its economic policy broke down whatever beginnings there were of an indigenous industrial development and promoted the proliferations of speculators, petty businessmen,

2 Paul A. Baran, *The Political Economy of Growth* (New York: Monthly Review Press, 1962), p. 145.

3 Ibid.

4 Brooks Adams, *The Law of Civilization and Decay, An Essay on History* (New York: 1896); quoted in Baran, op. cit., p. 146.

5 John Strachey, "Famine in Bengal" in Robert Lekachman, ed., *The Varieties of Economics* vol. 1 (New York: Meridian, 1962), p. 296.

> agents, and sharks of all descriptions eking out a sterile and precarious livelihood in the meshes of a decaying society.[6]

It was only later, however, after the period of extensive railroad construction, which began in 1857, that the British thoroughly penetrated the interior of India. British investors who sank money into these railroads were guaranteed a 5 percent return by the government which enforced a provision that if profits fell below 5 percent, the Indian people would be taxed to make up the difference. Thus, Indians were taxed to ensure that British investors would have adequate transport for the further economic exploitation of the Indian interior.

Despite such harsh measures, the age of European imperialism really did not get under way on a broad, pervasive front until the last quarter of the nineteenth century. Between 1775 and 1875, the European countries had lost about as much colonial territory as they had won. The opinion was widely held that colonies were expensive luxuries.

All this changed suddenly and drastically after 1875. By 1900, Great Britain had grabbed 4,500,000 square miles, which she added to her empire; France had gobbled up 3,500,000; Germany, 1,000,000; Belgium, 900,000; Russia, 500,000; Italy, 185,000; and the United States, 125,000. Imperialism ran rampant as one-fourth of the world's population was subjugated and put under European and American domination.

IMPERIALISM IN AFRICA

By 1800, the Europeans had hardly penetrated beyond the coastal areas of Africa. By the early twentieth century, after a 100-year orgy of land-grabbing and empire-building, they controlled over 10 million square miles, or about 93 percent of the continent. In that gigantic rape, various European powers sought to acquire the abundant minerals and agricultural commodities of the Dark Continent.

The brutality of the European exploitation of Africa was perhaps the most severe in the Belgian Congo. Belgian King Leopold II had sent H. M. Stanley into central Africa in 1879. Serving a private, profit-seeking company headed by Leopold and some of his associates, Stanley had a network of trading posts constructed and also duped native chiefs into signing "treaties" that established a commercial empire stretching over 900,000 square miles. Leopold set himself up as sovereign ruler of the Congo Free State and proceeded to exploit the natural and human resources of the area for the profits of his company.

[6] Baran, op. cit., p. 149.

The exploitation was ruthless. Natives were forced, through outright physical coercion, to gather rubber from the wild rubber trees and ivory from the elephants. Leopold confiscated all land that was not directly cultivated by the natives and placed it under "government ownership." Atrocities of the worst sort were committed to force the natives to submit to a very burdensome tax system which included taxes payable in rubber and ivory as well as in labor obligations.

By the twentieth century, the Congo had also become a rich source of diamonds, uranium, copper, cotton, palm oil, palm kernels, and coconuts. In general, it can be said that the Congo was one of the most profitable of European imperialistic exploits as well as one of the most scandalous.

The British grabbed the most populous and also the richest holdings in Africa. In 1870, Cecil Rhodes went to South Africa for his health. Within two years, his genius for organizing and controlling joint-stock companies and his ability to corner the market on diamonds had made him a millionaire. In later years, the British South Africa Company, which Rhodes headed, came to control South Africa completely. Although a private, profit-seeking company, it had all the power of a government, including the authority (given in its charter of 1889) to "make treaties, promulgate laws, preserve the peace, maintain a police force, and acquire new concessions."

The expansionist policies of the British South Africa Company led to the Boer War (1899–1902), which crushed the Dutch republics (the Orange Free State and the Transvaal republic) and gave Britain complete control over all South Africa. South Africa proved to be a rich mining region. But the legacy of British and Dutch imperialism is most vividly seen today in the suppression of the blacks who constitute the vast majority of the population.

The other instances of imperialism in Africa are no less deserving of study. It most suffice in this short account, however, to mention that on the eve of World War I, France held about 40 percent of Africa (much of it within the Sahara desert), England controlled 30 percent and the remaining roughly 23 percent was divided among Germany, Belgium, Portugal, and Spain.

IMPERIALISM IN ASIA

The results of the British take-over of India were evident by the turn of the twentieth century. In 1901, the per capita income was less than $10 per year; over two-thirds of the population were badly undernourished; most native Indian manufacturing had been either ruined or taken over by the British. Nearly 90 percent of the population struggled to subsist in villages where the average holding was only 5 acres and where farming techniques were primitive. Much of the meager produce was paid out in taxes, rents, and profits which accrued to the British. Famine, disease, and misery were rife. In 1891, the average Indian lived less than 26 years and usually died in misery.

Much of the rest of Asia was also subjugated during this period. In 1878, the British overran Afghanistan and placed it under the Indian government, and in 1907, Persia was divided between Russia and Britain.

In 1858, the French had used the murder of a Spanish missionary as the rationalization for invading Annam, a tributary state of China. They soon established a French colony in what is now Vietnam. With this toehold, the French succeeded, through war and intrigue, in bringing all the territory of Indochina under their domination by 1887.

The Malay Peninsula and the Malay Archipelago (which stretches for nearly 3,000 miles) were also carved up. The British grabbed Singapore and the Malay States, the northern part of Borneo, and southern New Guinea. Another part of New Guinea was taken by the Germans, and most of the remaining islands (an area comprising about 735,000 square miles) went to the Dutch.

american imperialism

Throughout much of the nineteenth century, American imperialism channeled all its energies in conquering the continent and exterminating the native American Indian population. The Samoa Islands were America's first overseas imperialist grab. In 1878, the natives of Pago Pago granted the Americans the right to use their harbor. Eleven years later, the islands had been conquered and divided between the United States and Germany.

Similarly, Pearl Harbor, in the Hawaiian Islands, became a U.S. naval station in 1887. It was but a very short time before American capitalists controlled most of Hawaii's sugar production. The tiny minority of white Americans soon revolted against Queen Liliuokalani's rule and, with the help of U.S. Marines, subjugated the native population. In 1898, Hawaii was officially annexed by the United States.

It was also in 1898 that the United States used the convenient sinking of the battleship *Maine* as an excuse to declare war on Spain and "liberate" the Cubans from Spanish oppression. Recognizing that it was no match for the United States, the Spanish government accepted every American demand, but the United States declared war anyway as a "measure of atonement" for the *Maine.* The American victory gave her Puerto Rico, Guam, and the Philippine

Islands outright, and the newly "independent" Cubans soon found American capitalists taking over most of their agriculture and commerce. Cuban independence had been restricted by a provision that the United States could intervene at its own discretion into Cuba's internal affairs "for the protection of life, property and individual liberty," a slogan that has been used to justify imperialism more than a few times. American troops invaded Cuba in 1906, 1911, and 1917, before secure control was finally established.

The Filipinos, who had been fighting for their independence from Spain, discovered the American brand to be no better than Spanish domination. President McKinley had decided that Americans were obligated "to educate the Filipinos and uplift and Christianize them," but the Filipinos, who had been Roman Catholics for centuries, resisted this American "Christianization." It took 60,000 American troops, as well as endless atrocities and concentration camps, before the Filipinos were finally "uplifted" and "educated."

In 1901, when the republic of Colombia refused to sell a strip of land (on which the Panama Canal was to be constructed) to the United States, President Roosevelt took action. A Panamanian insurrection was organized with American approval and help. United States warships were strategically placed to prevent Colombian troops from moving in to suppress the rebellion. The revolt started on November 3, 1903; on November 6, the United States extended diplomatic recognition to the "new nation"; on November 18, the United States had the Canal Zone on much more favorable terms than they had originally offered.

In 1904, President Roosevelt announced that the United States believed in the principle of self-determination for nations that acted "with reasonable efficiency and decency in social and political matters." He added, however, that "chronic wrongdoing, or any impotence which results in a general loosening of the ties of civilized society, may in America, as elsewhere, ultimately require intervention by some civilized nation. . . ."[7]

In 1909, U.S. Marines invaded Nicaragua to overthrow José Santos Zelaya, who had threatened American economic concessions there. In 1912, American troops were back in Nicaragua again. In 1915, American Marines invaded Haiti, and in 1916, American troops overwhelmed the Dominican Republic and established a military government there.

By World War I, the United States had seized or otherwise controlled Samoa, Midway Island, Hawaii, Puerto Rico, Guam, the Philippines, the island of Tutuila, Cuba, Santo Domingo, Haiti, Nicaragua, and the Panama Canal Zone.

[7] Quoted in G. C. Fite and J. E. Reese, *An Economic History of the United States* (2d ed.; Boston: Houghton Mifflin, 1965), p. 472.

imperialism and evolutionary socialism

The Boer War jolted British public opinion and resulted in strong conflicts among many radicals and socialists. On the one hand, it produced an abundance of jingoist sentiment and imperialist ideology that influenced some socialists, but on the other, J. A. Hobson's *Imperialism: A Study* caustically ridiculed this sentiment and ideology and advanced a theory of imperialism that was to have a profound influence on Marxists and many non-Marxist socialists.

Imperialism, according to Hobson, was a struggle for political and economic domination of areas of the world occupied by "lower races." Its "economic tap-root" was the necessity for advanced capitalist countries to find markets for the goods and capital produced domestically but for which there was inadequate domestic demand. Evoking traditions of nationalism and militarism, it could "appeal to the lust of quantitative acquisitiveness and of forceful domination surviving in a nation from early centuries of animal struggle for existence."[8]

The basic cause of the deficiency in domestic demand was, Hobson believed, a severely inequitable distribution of income which resulted in a distorted allocation of resources which led in turn to the quest for foreign markets. Hobson argued that the imperialist tendencies of the late nineteenth and early twentieth centuries could be reversed only by reform radical enough to effect a more equitable distribution of income. He summarized his position succinctly in the following passage:

> There is no necessity to open up new foreign markets; the home markets are capable of indefinite expansion. Whatever is produced in England can be consumed in England, provided that the "income," or power to demand commodities, is properly distributed. This only appears untrue because of the unnatural and unwholesome specialization to which this country has been subjected, based upon a bad distribution of economic resources, which has induced an overgrowth of certain manufacturing trades for the express purpose of effecting foreign sales. If the industrial revolution had taken place in an England founded upon equal access by all classes to land, education and legislation, specialization in manufactures would not have gone so far. . . . ; foreign trade would have been less important though more steady; the standard of life for all portions of the

[8] Quotations in this paragraph from J. A. Hobson, *Imperialism: A Study* (London: Allen and Unwin, 1938 [first published in 1902]), p. 368.

> population would have been high, and the present rate of national consumption would probably have given full, constant, remunerative employment to a far larger quantity of private and public capital than is now being employed.[9]

The issue of whether publicly to denounce English imperialism bitterly divided the Fabians. Sydney Olivier's insistence that the society's executive committee issue a pronouncement condemning the Boer War in particular and imperialism in general was rejected by one vote, but the committee agreed to the demand that the issue be put to a general vote.

Led by George Bernard Shaw, the proimperialist faction argued that small, backward nations could not manage their own affairs and should not be considered as nations at all and that the advanced European nations thus had a duty to police and manage the internal affairs of these backward peoples—for their own welfare. The debate was bitter. Finally, 45 percent of the membership voted to condemn English imperialism, and 55 percent opted to approve of or ignore imperialism. Immediately, 18 members of the society, including several of its most prominent personalities, handed in their resignations.

The sentiments of the German revisionists were similar to those of the Fabians, the majority either approving of European imperialism or not considering it a proper issue upon which to take a stand. Bernstein, for example, wrote: "only a conditional right of savages to the land occupied by them can be recognized. The higher civilization ultimately can claim a higher right."[10] Orthodox Marxists, however, were virtually unanimous in condemning imperialism which they analyzed as only the latest stage in the historical development of capitalism: Capitalists were forced by the mounting contradictions of the economic system to turn frantically to economic exploitation of more backward areas.

lenin's analysis of imperialism

The most famous and influential socialist analysis was contained in Lenin's pamphlet *Imperialism: The Highest Stage of Capitalism,* published in 1916. Lenin attempted "to show, as briefly and as popularly as possible, the principal economic characteristics of imperialism."[11] The most important was that in the imperialistic phase

[9] Ibid., pp. 88–89.

[10] Bernstein, op. cit., p. 179.

[11] *Imperialism: The Highest Stage of Capitalism* (London: Lawrence & Wishart, 1939), p. 1.

of capitalist development, the capitalist economies were thoroughly dominated by monopolies, a development that Marx had correctly foreseen. By monopolies, Lenin did not mean industries that consisted of only one firm (the modern economic definition of monopoly), but rather he referred to industries dominated by trusts, cartels, combinations, or by a few large firms.

Drawing heavily on the German experience, Lenin argued that the development of monopolies was closely related to important changes in the banking system. Banks had assumed a position of central importance in the drive toward cartelization and had come to exercise considerable control over many of the most important industrial cartels. This control was so extensive that Lenin spoke of the imperialistic phase of capitalism as the age of "finance capital."

Banks were able to mobilize huge sums of money for investment, but persistent downward pressures on domestic profit rates dictated that investment outlets be sought outside the home country. Lenin, unlike Hobson, did not believe that the necessity to export commodities was the most important economic cause of imperialism. Rather, it was the necessity to export capital. Backward areas offered a large and inexpensive labor force and lucrative investment prospects.

In the imperialist phase of capitalism, the various governments fought to gain access to privileged and protected markets for the combines and cartels within their own political boundaries. At the same time, these national combines and cartels sought to partition the world markets through international cartels. Deep-seated rivalry and competition, however, were more important than the opportunistic short-run collaborations. Persistent national conflicts and wars were the inevitable result. In Lenin's words:

> The epoch of the newest capitalism shows us that certain relations are being established between capitalist combines, *based* on the economic division of the world; while parallel with this and in connection with it, certain relations are being established between political alliances, between states, on the basis of the territorial division of the world, of the struggle for colonies, of the "struggle for economic territory."[12]

Such a situation was, Lenin believed, inherently unstable. Imperialism would lead to wars among the advanced capitalist countries and to rebellions and revolutions in the exploited areas. As long as the capitalist system could support its imperialistic thrust, however, it would prolong its existence by providing outlets for excess investment funds. The extra profits that imperialism secured

12 Ibid., p. 69.

for the home country meant that wages paid its workers could be raised. Thus, because it shared in the spoils, labor would at least temporarily be sapped of its revolutionary potential and controlled by right-wing labor leaders, "justly called social imperialists."[13]

If imperialism expanded the domain of capitalism and in doing so prolonged the system's existence, the tensions and conflicts it engendered were, Lenin believed, more severe than those of the competitive capitalism about which Marx wrote. Capitalism was still doomed, and socialism was still the wave of the future.

summary

During the late nineteenth and early twentieth centuries, workingmen made important economic and political gains throughout the capitalist world. This led many socialists to believe that capitalism could be transformed into socialism through gradual, peaceful political reform.

The same period witnessed the imperialistic carving-up of most of the world's economically underdeveloped areas. The inhabitants of these areas were harshly and cruelly exploited for the profits of large corporations in the advanced capitalist countries.

The issue of imperialism split the evolutionary socialist movement. Many of the reform socialists, for example, George Bernard Shaw and Eduard Bernstein, were strongly proimperialist. Others, among them J. A. Hobson, were strongly antiimperialist as were virtually all the Marxist socialists. Lenin's *Imperialism: The Highest Stage of Capitalism* was the most influential Marxist condemnation of imperialism.

[13] Ibid., p. 99.

chapter 10
keynesian economics and the great depression

While the period from the Civil War to 1900 was one of rapid economic expansion in the United States, these accomplishments were dwarfed by the growth from 1900 to 1929. The following figures show the percentage increase in value added by manufacture in several key industries between 1899 and 1927.[1]

Chemicals, etc.	239%
Leather and products	321%
Textiles and products	449%
Food products	551%
Machinery	562%
Paper and printing	614%
Steel and products	780%
Transportation and equipment	969%

In 1900, it has been estimated, U.S. wealth (the market values of all economic assets) was $86 billion; in 1929, it was $361 billion.

This spectacular growth gave the United States a huge edge over all other countries in manufacturing output. The American prosperity of the 1920s was based on high and rising levels of output.

[1] Figures taken from Leo Huberman, *We the People* (New York: Monthly Review Press, 1964), p. 254.

Real gross national product (GNP), adjusted for price changes, increased by 62 percent from 1914 to 1929. Only 3.2 percent of the labor force was unemployed in 1929, and labor productivity rose during that decade at least as fast as wages. Between 1921 and 1929, total automobile registrations increased from less than 11 to more than 26 million; consumers spent tens of millions of dollars on radios, refrigerators, and other electric appliances that had not been available before. American manufacturing seemed, to most, to be a permanent cornucopia destined to create affluence for all.

This leadership in manufacturing was associated with financial leadership in the world economy. The American economic empire began to rival that of England. By 1930, American businessmen owned large investments around the world. The following figures give the values of these investments in 1930:[2]

Canada	$3,942,000,000
Europe	4,929,000,000
Mexico and Central America	1,000,000,000
South America	3,042,000,000
West Indies	1,233,000,000
Africa	118,000,000
Asia	1,023,000,000
Oceania	419,000,000

the great depression

But this era of rapid growth and economic abundance came to a halt on October 24, 1929. On that "Black Thursday," the New York stock market saw security values begin a downward plummet that eventually was to destroy all confidence in business. Their confidence undermined, businessmen cut back production and investment. This decreased national income and employment, which, in turn, worsened business confidence even more. Before the process came to an end, thousands of corporations had gone bankrupt, millions were unemployed, and one of the worst national catastrophes in history was under way.

Between 1929 and 1932, there were over 85,000 business failures; more than 5,000 banks suspended operations; stock values on the New York Exchange fell from $87 billion to $19 billion; unemployment rose to 12 million, with nearly one-fourth of the population having no means of sustaining themselves; farm income fell by more than

2 Ibid., p. 251.

half; and manufacturing output decreased by almost 50 percent.[3]

America had plunged from the world's most prosperous country to one in which tens of millions lived in desperate, abject poverty. Particularly hard-hit were the blacks and other minority groups. The proportion of blacks among the unemployed was from 60 to 400 percent higher than the proportion of blacks in the general population.[4] Certain geographical areas suffered more than others. Congressman George Huddleston of Alabama reported in January 1932:

> We have about 108,000 wage and salary workers in my district. Of that number, it is my belief that not exceeding 8,000 have their normal incomes. At least 25,000 men are altogether without work. Some of them have not had a stroke of work for more than 12 months, maybe 60,000 or 75,000 are working one to five days a week, and practically all have had serious cuts in their wages and many of them do not average over $1.50 a day.[5]

Many cities reported that they could give relief payments for only a very short time, often one week, before people were forced to their own devices to subsist. The executive director of the Welfare Council of New York City described the plight of the unemployed.

> when the breadwinner is out of a job he usually exhausts his savings if he has any. Then, if he has an insurance policy, he probably borrows to the limit of its cash value. He borrows from his friends and from his relatives until they can stand the burden no longer. He gets credit from the corner grocery store and the butcher shop, and the landlord foregoes collecting the rent until interest and taxes have to be paid and something has to be done. All of these resources are finally exhausted over a period of time, and it becomes necessary for these people, who have never before been in want, to ask for assistance.
>
> The specter of starvation faces millions of people who have never before known what it was to be out of a job for any considerable period of time and who certainly have never known what it was to be absolutely up against it.[6]

The abject despair of these millions of people is at best suggested by a 1932 report describing the unloading of garbage in the Chicago

3 Figures taken from Louis M. Hacker, *The Course of American Economic Growth and Development* (New York: Wiley, 1970), pp. 300–301.

4 See Lester V. Chandler, *America's Greatest Depression* (New York: Harper & Row, 1970), pp. 40–41.

5 U.S., Congress, Senate Hearings before a subcommittee of the Committee on Manufactures, 72d Cong., 1st sess., p. 239.

6 Quoted in Chandler, op. cit., pp. 41–42.

city garbage dumps: "Around the truck which was unloading garbage and other refuse were about 35 men, women and children. As soon as the truck pulled away from the pile all of them started digging with sticks, some with their hands, grabbing bits of food and vegetables."[7]

What had happened to reduce the output of goods and services so drastically? Natural resources were still as plentiful as ever. The nation still had as many factories, tools, and machines. The people had the same skills and wanted to put them to work. And yet millions of workers and their families begged, borrowed, stole, and lined up for a pittance from charity, while thousands of factories stood idle or operated at far below capacity. The explanation lay within the institutions of the capitalist market system. Factories could have been opened and men put to work, but they were not because it was *not profitable* for businessmen to do this. And in a capitalist economy, production decisions are based primarily on the criterion of profits—not on peoples' needs.

the economics of keynes

The socialist cause gained many enthusiasts in the 1930s. While the capitalist world was suffering what was, perhaps, its most severe depression, the Soviet economy was experiencing rapid growth. When the depression struck, it was a traumatic shock to many Americans, who had come to believe that their country was destined to achieve unparalleled and unending increases in material prosperity.

The capitalist economic system seemed to be on the verge of total collapse. Drastic countermeasures were essential, but before the system could be saved, the malady had to be better understood. And to that task came one of the most brilliant economists of this century: John Maynard Keynes (1883–1946). In his famous book *The General Theory of Employment, Interest and Money,* Keynes attempted to show what had happened to capitalism so that it could be preserved.

Keynes began his analysis by looking at the process of production. In a given production period, a firm produces a certain dollar volume of goods. From the proceeds of the sale of these goods, the firm pays its costs of production which include wages, salaries, rent, supplies and raw materials, and interest on borrowed funds. What remains after these costs are paid is profit.

[7] Quoted in Huberman, op. cit., p. 260.

The important point to remember is this: What is a cost of production to the business firm represents income to an individual or another firm. The profit is also income—the income going to the owners of the firm. Because the value of production is exhausted by the costs of production and profits, and all these are income, it follows that the value of what has been produced must be equal to the incomes generated in producing it.

In terms of the entire economy, the aggregate picture is the same as that for the individual firm: The value of everything produced in the economy during any period is equal to the total of all incomes received in that period. Therefore, in order for businesses to sell all that they have produced, people must spend in the aggregate all their incomes. If an amount equal to the total income in society is spent on goods and services, then the value of production is realized in sales. In that case, profits remain high, and businessmen are willing to produce the same amount or more in the succeeding period.

Keynes called this a *circular flow:* Money flows from businesses to the public in the form of wages, salaries, rents, interest, and profits; this money then flows back to the businesses when the public buys goods and services from them. As long as businesses sell all they have produced and make satisfactory profits, the process continues.

But this does not happen automatically. When money flows from businesses to the public, some of it does not flow directly back to the businesses. The circular flow has leakages. To begin with, all people do not spend all their incomes. A percentage is saved, usually put into banks, and therefore withdrawn from the spending stream. This saving may be offset by other persons who borrow money from banks and spend more than their income. Keynes, however, pointed out that at the peak of prosperity, saving is usually greater than consumer borrowing; thus, there is usually net saving, or a net leakage, from circular income-expenditure flow.

Keynes also identified two other leakages. (1) People buy goods and services from foreign businesses, but the money spent on these imports cannot be spent on domestically produced goods. (2) The taxes people pay are also withdrawn from the income-expenditure flow.

These three leakages (saving, imports, and taxes) may be offset by three spending injections into the income-expenditure flow. (1) Imports can be offset by exports. They are exactly offset when foreigners buy goods produced in the United States in amounts equal to foreign imports purchased by Americans. (2) The government uses taxes to finance the purchase of goods and services. If it uses all taxes for this purpose and balances the budget, then government expenditures will exactly offset taxes in the spending stream. (3) If businessmen wish to expand their capital, they can finance investment in capital goods by borrowing the funds that were saved. Investment, then, may exactly offset the saving leakage.

If these three injections into the income-expenditure flow are just as large as the three leakages, then spending equals the value of production. Everything that has been produced can be sold, and prosperity reigns.

Keynes, however, believed that it was unlikely that the process could continue uninterrupted for very long. Investment, which is necessary to absorb savings, enlarges the capital stock and hence increases the economy's productive capacity. In order to utilize the new productive capacity fully, production and income must increase in the next period. But with the higher income, there will be more saving, which necessitates more investment, and this investment is by no means automatically forthcoming.

Keynes saw that those individuals with higher incomes saved a higher percentage of their incomes than those with low incomes. He concluded that this pattern would also hold for all society. As the aggregate income of society increases, the total savings increases more than proportionately. In other words, at each new higher level of income, a larger percentage of income is saved.

Thus, investment would have to increase at a faster rate than income if it were to continually offset saving. Only this rapid increase would permit businesses to sell everything they produced, but the faster investment grows, the more rapid is the increase in productive capacity. Because of this, the economy must invest even-greater amounts (both absolutely and relatively) in each successive period if the balance is to be maintained. In any mature private-enterprise economy, however, according to Keynes, the number of profitable investment outlets is limited. Hence, as the process of economic growth continues, the difficulty of finding sufficient investment outlets becomes more and more acute.

If it becomes impossible to find enough investment outlets, then investment falls short of saving, and the total expenditures for goods and services fall short of the value of those produced. Businesses, unable to sell all they have produced, find that their inventories of unsold goods are increasing. Each business sees only its own problem: that it has produced more than it can sell. It, therefore, reduces production in the next period. Most businesses, being in the same situation, do the same thing. The results are a large reduction of production, a decrease in employment, and a decline in income. With the decline in income, however, even less will be spent on goods and services in the next period. So businessmen again find that even at the lower level of production, they are unable to sell all they have produced. They again cut back production, and the downward spiral continues.

Under these circumstances, businesses have little or no incentive to expand their capital goods (because excess capacity already exists), and therefore investment falls drastically. Expenditures of all types plummet. As income declines, saving declines more than proportionately. This process continues until the declines in income have reduced saving to the point where it no longer exceeds the reduced level of investment. At this low level of income, equilibrium is restored. Leakages from the income-expenditure flow are again equal to the injections into it. The economy is stabilized, but at a level where high unemployment and considerable unused productive capacity exist.

Keynes' analysis was not, in its essentials, drastically different from those offered by Marx (Chapter 6) and Hobson (Chapter 9). The principal cause of a depression was, in the opinion of all three thinkers, the inability of capitalists to find sufficient investment opportunities to offset the increasing levels of saving generated by economic growth. Keynes' unique contribution was to show how the relation of saving to income could lead to a stable but depressed level of income, with widespread unemployment.

Marx (and Lenin) had believed the disease to be incurable. Hobson had prescribed measures to equalize the distribution of income and thereby reduce saving as a cure. Could Hobson's prescription work? This probably is not a very meaningful question. In most industrial capitalist countries, wealth and economic power determine political power, and those who wield power have never been willing to sacrifice it to save the economic system.

In the United States, for example, out of 300,000 nonfinancial corporations existing in 1925, the largest 200 made considerably more profit than the other 299,800 combined. The wealthiest 5 percent of the population owned virtually all the stocks and bonds and received in excess of 30 percent of the income. Needless to say, this 5 percent dominated American politics. In these circumstances, speculating about what would happen if the income and wealth were radically redistributed amounts to mere fanciful daydreaming.

Keynes' answer to the problem was more realistic. Government could step in when saving exceeded investment, borrow the excess saving, then spend the money on socially useful projects. They would be chosen in order not to increase the economy's productive capacity or decrease the investment opportunities of the future. This government spending would increase the injections into the spending stream and create a full-employment equilibrium. In doing so, it would not add to the capital stock. Therefore, unlike investment spending, it would not make a full-employment level of production more difficult to attain in the next period. Keynes summarized his position thus:

> Ancient Egypt was doubly fortunate, and doubtless owed to this its fabled wealth, in that it possessed *two* activities, namely, pyramid-building as well as the search for precious metals, the fruits of which, since they could not serve the needs of man by being consumed, did not stale with abundance. The Middle Ages built cathedrals and sang dirges. Two pyramids, two masses for the dead, are twice as good as one; but not so two railways from London to York.[8]

What type of expenditures ought the government to make? Keynes himself had a predilection toward useful public works such as the construction of schools, hospitals, parks, and other public conveniences. He realized, however, that this would probably benefit middle- and lower-income recipients much more than the wealthy. And because the wealthy have the political power, they would probably insist on policies that would not redistribute income away from them. He saw that it might be politically necessary to channel this spending into the hands of the large corporations, even though little that was beneficial to society would be accomplished directly. He wrote:

> If the Treasury were to fill old bottles with banknotes, bury them at suitable depths in disused coal-mines which are then filled up to the surface with town rubbish, and leave it to private enterprise on well-tried principles of laissez faire to dig the notes up again . . . there need be no more unemployment. . . . It would indeed be more sensible to build houses and the like; but if there are political and practical difficulties in the way of this, the above would be better than nothing.[9]

The depression of the 1930s dragged on until the outbreak of World War II. From 1936 (the year Keynes' *General Theory* was published) to 1940, economists hotly debated the merits of his theory and policy prescriptions. When the various governments began to increase armament production rapidly, however, unemployment began to melt away. During the war years, under the stimulus of enormous government expenditures, conditions in most capitalist economies were rapidly transformed from situations of severe unemployment to acute shortages of labor.

The American armed forces mobilized 14 million people who had to be armed, quartered, and fed. Between 1939 and 1944, the output of the manufacturing, mining, and construction industries doubled, and productive capacity increased by 50 percent. The American

[8] J. M. Keynes, *The General Theory of Employment, Interest and Money* (New York: Harcourt Brace Jovanovich, 1936), p. 131.

[9] Ibid., p. 129.

economy produced 296,000 planes, 5,400 cargo ships, 6,500 naval vessels, 64,500 landing craft, 86,000 tanks, and 2,500,000 trucks.[10] During the war period, the most pressing problem was a *shortage* of labor, as contrasted with the 19 percent unemployment that existed as late as the beginning of 1939.

keynesian economics and ideology

Most economists believed that this wartime experience had proven the basic correctness of Keynes' ideas. Capitalism could be saved, they proclaimed, by the wise use of the government's powers to tax, borrow, and spend money. Capitalism was, again, a viable social and economic system.

But viability alone was insufficient as an ideology for capitalism. Russia had not experienced unemployment in the 1930s, and its spectacular rate of growth during this period had proven the viability of the soviet economic system. This challenge elicited a resurgence of the older neoclassical economic ideology. Older theories were cast in an esoteric and highly elaborate mathematical framework. Typical of these new economists was Paul A. Samuelson, whose book *The Foundations of Economic Analysis* is among the technically most formidable treatments of economics.[11] In 1947, The American Economic Association awarded him the first John Bates Clark Medal for the most outstanding contribution to economics made by an economist under forty years of age. The book was also instrumental in securing the Nobel Prize in economics for Samuelson in 1970.

Samuelson has made an even more significant contribution in terms of his influence on the dominant economic ideology of capitalism in the last 25 years. His introductory text, *Economics,* which has undergone eight editions, has been translated into almost every major language, and has sold millions of copies.[12] The first edition set out mainly to explain and simplify Keynes' ideas. Each subsequent edition has tended to bring in more of the traditional neoclassical ideology of capitalism. In 1955, Samuelson offered his "grand neoclassical synthesis," an integration of Keynesian with neoclassical economics. The Keynesian theory would provide the knowledge necessary to maintain a full-employment economy, and the market system could operate within this Keynesian framework to

10 All figures taken from Hacker, op. cit., p. 325.

11 Paul A. Samuelson, *The Foundations of Economic Analysis* (Cambridge, Mass.: Harvard University Press, 1947).

12 Paul A. Samuelson, *Economics* (New York: McGraw-Hill, 1948).

allocate resources according to the time-honored principles of the neoclassical ideology.

Almost every student of economics for the last 25 years has learned his elementary economics from Samuelson's text, or from one of the many others that have attempted to copy his approach and content.

the efficacy of keynesian economic policies

After 1945, Keynesian economics became orthodoxy for both economists and the majority of politicians. Almost 3 million veterans were demobilized in that year. In 1946, another 11 million joined the civilian labor force. Congress and many economists feared a new depression and immediately took steps to apply the new Keynesian ideas. Passage of the Employment Act of 1946 legally obligated the government to use its taxing, borrowing, and spending powers to maintain full employment. The act declared that "It is the continuing policy and responsibility of the Federal government to use all practicable means . . . for the purpose of creating and maintaining . . . conditions under which there will be afforded useful employment opportunities, including self-employment, for those able, willing, and seeking to work, and to promote maximum employment, production and purchasing power."

Have Keynesian economic policies worked? The answer to this question is very complex. Since World War II, there have been no major depressions in the United States, but there have been five "recessions" (the modern euphemism for a mild depression). In 1948–1949, a recession lasted for 11 months; in 1953–1954, for 13 months; in 1957–1958, for 9 months; and in 1960–1961, for 9 months. As of this writing, the 1969–1971 recession has been going on for over two years.

Because of recessions, the economy's performance in the 1950s left much to be desired. The real rate of growth of GNP was 2.9 percent, which does not compare very favorably with the 4.7 percent for 1920–1929 or the 3.7 percent for 1879–1919. The brightest spot in the American economy's performance has been the growth rate in the 1960s, which averaged around 5 percent.

Unemployment for the 1950s and early 1960s averaged 4.6 percent, although it dipped to 3.5 percent in the mid-1960s. Moreover, inflation has been a persistent problem since World War II. From 1945 through 1968, the average annual increase in wholesale prices was 3.8 percent (most of which occurred in the late 1940s); the rate of increase from 1968 to 1970 was nearly 5 percent. The 1969–1971 inflation was accompanied by an economic recession in which unemployment soared to rates of over 6 percent. The simultaneous occurrence of both high unemployment and a high rate of inflation led to President Nixon's attempt to freeze wages and prices in late 1971, followed by the "phase II" plan for government control over increases in wages and prices.

On balance, Keynesian policies appear to have worked with moderate success. Before judging this performance, however, it is necessary to see what the American government substituted for the pyramids of Egypt and the cathedrals of the Middle Ages. In 1960, one observer wrote: "A central aspect of our growth experience of the past two decades is one which few spokesmen for the future candidly discuss. This is the fact that our great boom did not begin until the onset of World War II, and that its continuance since then has consistently been tied to a military rather than to a purely civilian economic demand."[13]

the warfare economy

In 1940, military and military-related expenditures were $3.2 billion, or 3.2 percent of GNP. By 1947, they were still only $9.1 billion, or 3.9 percent of GNP. From that time onward, the amount spent on militarism grew steadily and rapidly. By 1960, military expenditures were 8.9 percent of GNP. During the rapid growth of the 1960s, military expenditures grew at approximately the same rate as GNP. If other expenses that are related to militarism but not included in the "defense" budget are taken into account, the total has been close to 15 percent in recent years.[14] The United States has spent and continues to spend more on militarism than any other country—more in absolute terms, relative terms, and per capita.

The result of these enormous expenditures has been the growth of the *military-industrial complex* as a necessary adjunct to economic prosperity. Its essential features have been described as follows:

> The warfare state we have constructed over the last two generations has a large clientele. At the top of the pyramid is the so-called military–industrial complex. It comprises, first, the Defense Department of the Federal Government, along with such satellites as the CIA and NASA. The admirals and generals, the

[13] Robert Heilbroner, *The Future as History* (New York: Harper & Row, 1960), p. 133.

[14] See, for example, Daniel R. Fusfeld, "Fascist Democracy in the United States," *Conference Papers of the Union for Radical Economics* (December 1968), pp. 11 and 34–35.

> space scientists and the intelligence men, like all government bureaucrats, are busily engaged in strengthening their influence. To this end they cultivate congressmen and senators, locate military establishments in politically strategic districts, and provide legislators with special favors. Former military men are drawn into the net of influence through the Army and Navy associations and through veterans' organizations.
>
> The military are supported by the industrial side of the complex. These are the large corporations on whom the military depend for the hardware of modern war. Some sell the bulk of their output to the military, like North American Aviation, Lockheed Aircraft, General Dynamics, McDonnell-Douglas, and Thiokol Chemical. Others are important military suppliers but make the bulk of their sales in civilian markets, such as Western Electric, Sperry Rand, General Electric, or IBM. Others, such as Dupont and General Motors, are only occasionally military contractors.[15]

The extent to which military production dominates the American economy is indicated by a recent survey which showed that five key military-related industries accounted for 7.9 percent of all employment in New York, 12.3 percent in New Jersey, 13 percent in Texas, 14.6 percent in Massachusetts, 15.7 percent in Maryland, 20.9 percent in Florida, 23.4 percent in Connecticut, 30 percent in Kansas, 31.4 percent in California, and 34.8 percent in Washington.[16]

Military expenditures operate in exactly the way Keynes believed pyramid-building operated in the ancient Egyptian economy. For generals and most politicians, a tenfold overkill potential is twice as good as a fivefold overkill; two ABM (antiballistic missile) systems are twice as good as one, but only half as good as four. And if the public cannot be easily convinced of this, the immense amount of research financed by the military-industrial complex comes to the fore. Weapons and delivery systems are rapidly superseded by new models. Horror stories convince the public that a further escalation of the arms race is necessary and that "obsolete" (and often unused) models must be scrapped.

Military spending keeps the capital-goods industry operating at near full capacity without raising the economy's productive capacity as rapidly as would be the case if they provided capital goods for industry. Demand does not tend to drop below supply as persistently as it formerly did; military spending increases demand without increasing productivity.

The neglect of these effects of the Keynesian military-induced prosperity is perhaps "the most important abdication of any by the

15 Ibid., p. 13.

16 Ibid., p. 15.

economists."[17] This type of economic theory has led to "an ahistorical, a technical or mechanical, a nonpolitical view of what the economy is and how it works."[18]

Very few Keynesian economists have been willing to come to grips with the implication of militarism as a tool of economic policy.

> The arms economy has been the major Keynesian instrument of our times. But its use has been cloaked as "national interest," its effects have been largely undermined, its international consequences largely deleterious and destabilizing, its importance making for uncritical acceptance and dependence by large segments of the society, its long-run effects hardly glanced at. The arms economy has done much more than distort the use of scarce creative scientific and engineering talent. . . . It has forced us to neglect a whole range of urgent social priorities, the consequences of which threaten the fabric of our society.[19]

summary

The severity of the Great Depression of the 1930s caused many economists to become dissatisfied with the orthodox neoclassical economists' view that unemployment was merely a short-run, ephemeral "adjustment" to a temporary disequilibrium situation. Keynes' new ideas were rapidly accepted by most important economists. World War II proved that massive government intervention in the market economy could create full employment, indeed, Hitler's Germany had already established this in the 1930s.

Since the war, the United States has not had a major depression. Most economists agree that massive government spending is largely responsible for this improved performance of American capitalism. Critics have argued, however, that the social price of this prolonged prosperity has been the creation of a military-industrial complex that currently threatens the entire fabric of American society.

If this view is correct, then it is possible to conclude that Keynes' theories did enable the neoclassical ideology to come to grips with the most important economic problem of the 1930s but have obscured if not worsened other problems. Some of these problems and some contemporary ideologies of capitalism will be examined in Chapter 11.

[17] Sumner M. Rosen, "Keynes Without Gadflies," in T. Roszak, ed., *The Dissenting Academy* (New York: Random House, Vintage Books, 1968), p. 83.

[18] Ibid., p. 85.

[19] Ibid., pp. 86–87.

chapter 11
contemporary american capitalism and its defenders

Since World War II, the American economy has experienced five mild recessions, albeit its growth has been fairly satisfactory by historical standards. Gross national product, in constant (1958) dollars, grew from $355 billion in 1950 to $727 billion in 1969. Disposable personal income, again in constant (1958) dollars, grew from $250 billion to $512 billion over the same period.[1] Judged by historical standards, this has certainly been a creditable performance.

The technological advances of American capitalism have been particularly impressive. For several decades prior to World War I, the increases in output per man-hour in American industry had been about 22 percent per decade. After World War II, output per man-hour increased by 35–40 percent per decade.[2] This growth has been made possible by huge expenditures on research and development, which increased from $3.4 billion in 1950 to $12 billion in 1960; fully one-half of these funds came from the federal government.

With these improvements in technology and increases in produc-

1 Figures taken from the *Federal Reserve Bulletin* (August 1970), pp. A68–A69.

2 Louis M. Hacker, *The Course of American Economic Growth and Development* (New York: Wiley, 1970), p. 326. The increases in productivity in the 1920s had been even more impressive, however.

tion has come a greater concentration of economic power in the hands of a very small number of corporations. In 1929, the 100 largest manufacturing corporations had legal control (actual control being far greater) of 44 percent of the net capital assets of all manufacturing corporations. By 1962, this figure had increased to 58 percent.[3]

In 1962, there were 420,000 manufacturing enterprises. But a mere 5 of these enterprises owned 12.3 percent of all manufacturing assets; 20 owned 25 percent of the total. The total assets of the 20 largest firms were approximately as large as those of the 419,000 smallest companies combined. These 20 giants took a whopping 38 percent of all after-tax profits, leaving the smallest 419,980 to divide 62 percent. Furthermore, of the 180,000 *corporations* involved in manufacturing, the net profits of the 5 largest were nearly twice as large as those of the 178,000 smallest corporations.[4]

The rate of concentration has quickened. In every year since 1959, there have been more than 60 mergers a year involving the acquisition of companies having over $10 million in assets. The number of mergers has increased throughout the sixties. Table 11.1 illustrates this trend.[5] From 1968 to 1970, the evidence points to an ever-faster rate of acquisition. The process of increasing economic concentration, which began about 100 years ago, continues unabated today.

TABLE 11.1

large mergers and acquisitions, 1966–1968

	1966	1967	1968
Total number of acquisitions	1,746	2,384	4,003
Number of acquired manufacturing and mining companies with more than $10 million assets	101	169	192
Value of assets of acquired companies with more than $10 million assets (in billions)	$4.1	$8.2	$12.6
Number of acquisitions made by 200 largest companies	33	67	74
Value of assets of companies acquired by 200 largest companies (in billions)	$2.4	$5.4	$6.9

[3] Gardiner C. Means, "Economic Concentration," in *Hearings before the Subcommittee on Antitrust and Monopoly of the Committee on the Judiciary, United States Senate* (Washington, D.C.: U.S. Government Printing Office, July 1964), pp. 9–19.

[4] Willard F. Mueller, "Economic Concentration," *Hearings,* op. cit., pp. 111–129.

[5] Table constructed from data of the Federal Trade Commission, derived by Paul Sweezy and Harry Magdoff, "The Merger Movement: A Study in Power," *The Monthly Review* (June 1969), pp. 1–5.

The post–World War II prosperity has not reduced the extremes of inequality in the United States. In the most complete study of the distribution of ownership of wealth ever undertaken,[6] it has been shown that the wealthiest 1.6 percent of the population owns over 80 percent of all corporate stock and virtually all state and local government bonds. Furthermore, the concentration of ownership of these income-yielding assets has steadily increased since the early 1920s.

The distribution of income reflects the same extreme inequality. Despite the economy's impressive growth over the past three decades—and the much-publicized war on poverty of the early 1960s, which proved to be a half-hearted minor skirmish—poverty has remained an acute problem in the United States. In 1970, for example, 25.5 million Americans lived in families that had an annual income of less than $3,900, the officially designated "poverty level."[7] The U.S. Bureau of Labor Statistics (BLS) reported that with the high prices that prevailed in 1970, it would require about $7,100 for a family of four to live with "a sense of self-respect and social participation."[8] Thus, most of these 25.5 million persons lived on less than one-half the amount necessary to generate "self-respect." Tens of millions more lived on less than $7,100.

In stark contrast to this widespread poverty, the wealthiest 5 percent of the American population received over 20 percent of all income. At the top of this 5 percent was the elite 1.6 percent that owns most of the income-yielding stocks and bonds in the United States. The richest of the elite had incomes estimated to be between $50 million and $100 million per year (the latter income is about $275,000 per day).

Furthermore, taxes do little, if anything, to reduce the inequities in the distribution of income. It is commonly supposed that the U.S. tax system reduces inequality by taking a higher percentage of the income of the wealthy than is taken from the poor. The personal income tax does tend to reduce income inequalities, but the effect is much smaller than most people imagine. When economists analyze the total tax burden, however, they find that taxes actually increase inequality in the distribution of income because sales taxes, excise taxes, property taxes, and social security taxes all take a much-larger percentage of the poor man's income than of the rich man's.

One economist, a recognized authority on taxes, has analyzed the

[6] Robert J. Lampman, *The Share of Top Wealth-holders in National Wealth, 1922–1956* (Princeton, N.J.: Princeton University Press, 1962).

[7] *Los Angeles Times,* May 8, 1971, part I, p. 1.

[8] Ibid., December 21, 1970, part I, p. 18.

total tax burden on incomes along the entire distribution spectrum. He found that families with incomes below $2,000 per year—certainly a level of abject poverty—paid out one-third of their incomes in taxes. As incomes got higher, people paid a lower percentage of their incomes in taxes. For example, families making between $10,000 and $15,000 paid a proportion of their income that was nearly one-third lower than that paid by families with incomes below $2,000. Only among the wealthiest 5 percent of families did the total tax bite exceed that exacted from the poorest. The wealthy elite actually paid out, on the average, 36.3 percent of their income for taxes, a mere 3 percent higher than the poorest segment of society paid.[9]

Thus, it appears that on the one hand, American capitalism in the last three decades has proven fairly successful if judged solely by the criteria of economic growth and productivity (although there has been persistent unemployment and inflation). On the other hand, the extreme inequalities in the distribution of wealth and income have continued and even grown worse. It is not surprising, therefore, that these decades have seen numerous ideological defenses of American capitalism as well as socialist and radical critiques of the U.S. economy.

contemporary classical liberal ideology

Neoclassical economics was the principal purveyor of the classical liberal ideology of capitalism during the late nineteenth and early twentieth centuries. Since the 1930s, neoclassical economics has become more and more complex mathematically, which has enabled modern economists to gain many new theoretical and scientific insights. Its most important assumptions, however, those on which the entire theory rests, are still metaphysical in character. They have not been established on a scientific basis, either empirically or theoretically.

The finest summary of contemporary neoclassical economics is C. E. Ferguson's *The Neoclassical Theory of Production and Distribution.*[10] The mathematical reasoning in this book is so complex that very few people other than professional economists who are thoroughly competent in higher mathematics can understand it. Professor Ferguson is aware, however, of the tenuous nature of many of the assumptions of this ideology, which, like the medieval religious

9 B. A. Musgrave, "Estimating the Distribution of the Tax Burden," In *Income and Wealth,* Series 10 (Cambridge, England: Bowes & Bowes, 1964), p. 192.

10 C. E. Ferguson, *The Neoclassical Theory of Production and Distribution* (London: Cambridge University Press, 1969).

ideology of feudalism, ultimately must be accepted on faith alone. He admits this and asserts his personal faith: ". . . placing reliance upon neoclassical economic theory is a matter of faith. I personally have the faith; but at present the best I can do to convince others is to invoke the weight of Samuelson's authority. . . ."[11]

When the thrust toward esoterica removed classical liberal ideology from the level at which it could be widely understood, however, it also substantially reduced its effectiveness as a popular ideology of capitalism. To promote the widespread popular acceptance of the ideology has been the task of numerous organizations. The best-known American organizations, which propagate a simplified, more popular version of the classical ideology, are the National Association of Manufacturers (NAM), the Foundation for Economic Education, the Committee for Constitutional Government, the United States Chamber of Commerce, and the American Enterprise Association.

A congressional committee found that of $33.4 million spent "to influence legislation," $32.1 million was spent by large corporations. And of this $32.1 million, about $27 million went to such organizations as those mentioned in the previous paragraph.[12] The NAM uses this money to publish a large amount of probusiness propaganda, including "an educational literature series, labor and industrial relations bulletins, news bulletins, a magazine of American affairs, and numerous studies on legislation, education, anti-trust laws, tariffs and unions."[13]

The Foundation for Economic Education reviews and distributes books that reflect the classical liberal ideology of capitalism and publishes and distributes, free of charge, a monthly journal, *The Freeman,* which propagates this ideology. The other organizations engage in numerous publishing and promotional activities designed to inculcate the same ideology as widely as possible.

The popularized statement of the classical ideology lays principal stress on the benefits of the free market. It is argued that the forces of supply and demand in a free market will always lead to results that are preferable to anything that could be achieved by the

[11] Ibid., pp. xvii–xviii. Professor Ferguson's candid admission was prompted by a rather esoteric debate among academic economists. They were debating what they called the "reswitching of productive techniques." The debate proved conclusively that some of the most fundamental tenets of neoclassical orthodoxy were untenable. For a summary of the conclusions of the debate, see E. K. Hunt, "Religious Parable Versus Economic Logic: An Analysis of the Recent Controversy in Value, Capital and Distribution Theory," *Inter-Mountain Economic Review* (Fall 1971), also see section III of E. K. Hunt and Jesse Schwartz, *Critique of Economic Theory* (London: Penguin, 1972).

[12] R. Joseph Monsen, Jr., *Modern American Capitalism* (Boston: Houghton Mifflin, 1963), p. 19.

[13] Ibid.

government or a central planning agency. The NAM, for example, asserts that the proper function of the government is to strengthen and "make more effective the regulation by competition."[14] Almost none of its literature, however, suggests much concern with the concentration of corporate power. Rather, the main economic problems are the powers of big labor unions and the "socialistic" welfare measures of the government.

In essence, most of this literature uses a drastically simplified version of some of the classical and neoclassical economists' analyses. It supports the view that any conceivable threat to the operation of the free market, whether real or potential, is an evil to be avoided at any cost. These organizations have had considerable success in propagating this point of view, particularly among small businessmen. (Big business, however, generally continues to look with favor on government intervention—because it usually benefits from such actions.)

contemporary variants of the classical liberal ideology

Most critics of the classical liberal ideology emphasize its failure to come to grips with the realities of the concentration of immense power in the hands of considerably less than 1 percent of the corporations. Several attempts have been made to construct an ideology that retains the competitive, private-enterprise flavor of classical liberalism while recognizing the existence of concentrated corporate power. Two of these will be discussed: the *countervailing power* ideology, associated primarily with the economist John Kenneth Galbraith, and the *people's capitalism* ideology, associated primarily with Professor Massimo Salvadori.

In his famous book *American Capitalism, the Concept of Countervailing Power,* Professor Galbraith recognized the existence of large, special-interest power blocks in the American economy, but argued then that they should not be of much concern because "private economic power begets the countervailing power of those who are subject to it."[15] The result of this newly created countervailing power is "the neutralization of one position of power by another."[16]

14 National Association of Manufacturers, Economic Principles Commission, *The American Individual Enterprise System, Its Nature and Future* (New York: McGraw-Hill, 1946), p. 57.

15 John Kenneth Galbraith, *American Capitalism, the Concept of Countervailing Power* (Boston: Houghton Mifflin, 1956), p. 4.

16 Ibid., p. 1.

Thus, strong unions neutralize strong business firms in the field of labor relations, and strong buyers' associations neutralize the monopolistic or oligopolistic powers of strong sellers. The result, then, is a kind of market equilibrium or invisible hand that harmonizes the interests of all. The harmonious whole is now simply made up of a few neutralized giants rather than numerous, atomistically competitive small firms.[17]

Another influential attempt to show the innocuous (or even beneficial) nature of corporate concentration was made by Professor Salvadori, who used the slogan "people's capitalism" to characterize what he believed to be the most essential feature of contemporary American capitalism: the diffusion of ownership. The widespread diffusion of ownership of corporate stock, as well as other types of assets, means, to Salvadori, that capitalism is no longer a system where a tiny minority reaps most of the privileges, but one in which the majority are rapidly becoming capitalists and getting a share of the privileges.[18] Salvadori has conveniently summarized his people's capitalism ideology:

> At present in the United States there are nearly half a million corporations; stockholders total about ten million (1959). Their numbers have increased rapidly in the post-war period. Standard Oil of New Jersey, for instance, had about 160,000 stockholders in 1946; twelve years later there were three times as many, close to half a million. As a rule, the larger the corporation the more widely spread the ownership. Large corporations in which a majority of shares are owned by an individual or by a family are fewer and fewer. It is already exceptional for a single individual to own more than four or five per cent of the stock of a given corporation. Unincorporated non-farm businesses number about four million; they belong to one or more individuals and this means millions of "capitalists." Nearly four million farmers (three-fourths of the total) are full owners or part owners of the farms they cultivate. Even considering that there is a good deal of overlapping among the three groups (shareholders, individual non-farm owners, farmers) one can say that at least one-fourth to one-third of all American families share the ownership of natural and artificial capital. There are also half a million independent professional

[17] It should be mentioned that Professor Galbraith has published several books since *American Capitalism, the Concept of Countervailing Powers* appeared. Even a cursory reading of these books shows that he has altered his opinions fundamentally. Nevertheless, because the countervailing power of ideology has been very influential, and because most of this influence flows from his book, we are justified in associating this ideology with his name.

[18] This is curiously similar to socialist Eduard Bernstein's idea, discussed in Chapter 9.

> people—lawyers, doctors, architects, engineers, accountants, etc.—whose other means of production are not only equipment of one kind or another but also skill and training, and whose income is related to the capital invested in acquiring professional efficiency; they are "capitalists" just as much as owners of natural and artificial capital. Most other families own durable consumer goods (houses, summer cottages, furniture, cars, electrical appliances, etc.), federal, state, and municipal bonds, insurance policies and savings to the extent that they can consider themselves "capitalists."[19]

Thus, bigness of corporations does not, for Salvadori, appear to be an issue. Ownership is becoming more equitably distributed because most people are becoming "capitalists," and hence, by implication, none is powerful enough to exploit another. Disciples point out that by 1970, there were approximately 30 million stockholders. In this view, the United States is becoming a nation where the majority are capitalists.

Even many defenders of capitalism concede that Salvadori's analysis serves only to obscure the nature of the concentration of economic power in the United States and that it neither eliminates nor justifies this concentration. A. A. Berle, Jr., a distinguished scholar of American capitalism as well as a corporation executive, has written:

> In terms of power, without regard to asset positions, not only do 500 corporations control two-thirds of the non-farm economy, but within each of that 500 a still smaller group has the ultimate decision-making power. That is, I think, the highest concentration of economic power in recorded history. . . . Since the United States carries on not quite half of the manufacturing production of the entire world today, these 500 groupings—each with its own little dominating pyramid within it—represents a concentration of power over economies which makes the medieval feudal system look like a Sunday school party.[20]

Contrary to the tone of this quotation, Berle is not a critic of American capitalism, but one of the most important developers of a contemporary corporate, or collective, ideology of capitalism.

19 Massimo Salvadori, *The Economics of Freedom* (Garden City, N.Y.: Doubleday 1959), pp. 70–71.

20 A. A. Berle, Jr., "Economic Power and the Free Society," in Andrew Hacker, ed., *The Corporation Take-Over* (Garden City, N.Y.: Doubleday, 1965), p. 97.

the contemporary corporate ethic and capitalist ideology

The tactics of the late nineteenth-century robber barons led most people to reject the corporate ideology (discussed in Chapter 8). Their destructive competition and financial wheeling and dealing hardly supported the conclusion that they were becoming socialized stewards of the public welfare. And yet the classical liberal ideology had no real defense for the existing concentration of economic and political power. The Christian corporate ethic, with its emphasis on the paternalistic benevolence of the powerful, was still the only successful ideological defense of great inequalities of wealth and power.

It was simply not credible to cast the nineteenth-century capitalist in a kindly, paternalistic role. But some twentieth-century ideologists of capitalism have argued that capitalism has changed so drastically that capitalists have lost their importance in the system and have been replaced by a new class of professional managers. These theories envision this "new man," the professional manager, as the paternalistic steward of public welfare.

In 1932, A. A. Berle and G. C. Means published an important and influential book, *The Modern Corporation and Private Property.*[21] In it, they argued that ownership of most of the colossal corporate giants had become so widely diffused that the owners of stock had lost or were rapidly losing control of these corporations. With no single owner holding more than 1 or 2 percent of the stock and with no effective ways of colluding, the owners were left with only the formal voting function when selecting the boards of directors. Candidates for whom they could vote were selected by the existing boards of directors. Thus, the boards chose their own replacements and were, essentially, a self-perpetuating oligarchy. They wielded power but had no necessary connection with the owners of stock. They were not capitalists in the usual sense of the term.

In 1955, Berle wrote another book, *The Twentieth Century Capitalist Revolution,* in which he argued that corporations had developed a quasipolitical status. Managers were primarily motivated by the desire to promote the general public interests in their decision-making, and any who were not so motivated would be forced by public opinion and the threat of government intervention so to act.

[21] A. A. Berle and G. C. Means, *The Modern Corporation and Private Property* (New York: Macmillan, 1932).

This view has been widely accepted. Another economist, for example, wrote:

> No longer the agent of proprietorship seeking to maximize return on investment, management sees itself as responsible to stockholders, employees, customers, the general public, and, perhaps most important, the firm as an institution. . . . There is no display of greed or graspingness; there is no attempt to push off onto workers or the community at large part of the social costs of the enterprise. The modern corporation is a soulful corporation.[22]

The corporation was "soulful," of course, because, in this economist's opinion, its managers were conscientious, paternalistic stewards of society's welfare.

The managerial ideology was spelled out in some detail in a series of lectures delivered by prominent corporation managers at Columbia University in 1956. According to the chairman of General Electric, the lectures were intended "to coax us businessmen out of our offices and into the arena of public thought where our managerial philosophies can be put to the test of examination by men trained in other disciplines."[23]

One of the dominant themes in these lectures was that because American capitalism is "new," the complaints men once may have had against capitalism are no longer justified. Thus, the chairman of Sears-Roebuck asserted: "The historic complaint that big business, as the producing arm of capitalism, exploited the many for the profit of the few and deprived the workers of the products of their own labor had a valid basis in the facts of European capitalism, but lacks substance when applied to American capitalism today."[24]

Another theme was the justification of bigness on the grounds of better efficiency and higher quality. "The American public," asserted the chairman of United States Steel, "has gradually become accustomed to larger and larger groups and has become convinced that big production groups are outstanding in reliability and in the quality of their products and services and are necessary to perform America's larger production tasks in research, in production, and in the procurement of raw materials."[25]

Finally, the businessmen all saw managers as "professional" men who are as much concerned with "customers, share owners,

[22] Carl Kaysen, "The Social Significance of the Modern Corporation," *American Economic Review* (May 1957), pp. 313–314.

[23] Quoted in Robert L. Heilbroner, *The Limits of American Capitalism* (New York: Harper & Row, 1966), p. 30.

[24] Ibid., pp. 31–32.

[25] Ibid., p. 32.

employees, suppliers, educational institutions, charitable activities, government and the general public" as they are with sales and profits. They believed that managers "all know that special power imposes special responsibilities on those who hold it." Most managers, they asserted, fully accept "their responsibilities for the broader public welfare."[26]

Since 1942, this corporate managerial ideology has been assiduously disseminated by the Committee for Economic Development (CED). The CED readily accepted big business and also "the fact that government was big and was constantly growing bigger and that there was no returning to a simpler, happier past in this respect. It believed that the question was not *how much* government should do, but *what* it should do."[27] Government should not only accept all the duties assigned to it by the classical liberal ideology but also follow Keynesian policies to ensure stable full employment. Further, government should cooperate with corporate management in resolving conflicts and maintaining the tranquil, stable atmosphere within which management can effectively perform its public-spirited, paternalistic functions of promoting the public welfare.[28]

Big business and big government are accepted by this ideology as not only inevitable but also necessary for maximum efficiency. Big labor unions are also accepted as long as they recognize that most of their legitimate interests are in harmony with the interests of business and management.

Another important propagator of the managerial ideology has been the United States Information Agency (USIA), the official government agency charged with the worldwide propagandizing of the "American point of view." The USIA operates on a grand scale. Its Voice of America broadcasts are heard around the world daily in scores of languages, and it publishes dozens of newspapers and magazines, maintains libraries, shows motion pictures, and engages in countless other propaganda operations.

Arthur Larson, who "was a semi-official ideologist to the Eisenhower Administration and a former head of the United States Information Agency,"[29] published a book, *What We Are For,*[30] in which he explained the philosophy of USIA propaganda. In the modern capitalist economy, Larson argued, the government should do only what "needs to be done" and cannot be done "as well" by

[26] Quotations in this paragraph are all from ibid., pp. 32–33.

[27] Karl Schriftgiesser, *Business Comes of Age* (New York: Harper & Row, 1960), p. 224.

[28] See Monsen, op. cit., pp. 25–29.

[29] Ibid., p. 42.

[30] Arthur Larson, *What We Are For* (New York: Harper & Row, 1959).

private businesses.[31] Modern capitalism has a plurality of powerful interest groups such as big business, big unions, big government, and so forth, which have no major or basic conflicts. Rather, their interests harmonize, and they mutually support each other. Larson assumed both that business managers are motivated primarily by the desire to promote social welfare to meet the "basic political and economic needs of all people,"[32] and that businesses operate more efficiently than government. There is, therefore, a built-in preference for a minimal role for government in the economy.[33]

criticisms of contemporary capitalist ideologies

Criticisms of capitalism have often gone hand in hand with criticisms of capitalist ideologies. In the remaining part of this chapter, criticisms of the ideologies of capitalism will be examined. Some of the principal criticisms of contemporary American capitalism will be discussed in Chapter 12.

CRITICISMS OF NEOCLASSICAL IDEOLOGY

Neoclassical economics completely dominated orthodox academic economics in the late nineteenth and early twentieth centuries. From the 1930s onward, however, it increasingly came under attack. In 1938, Oscar Lange and Fred M. Taylor published their significant book *On the Economic Theory of Socialism.*[34] Lange and Taylor accepted the neoclassical argument that a "purely" and "perfectly" competitive economy will lead to an "optimum allocation of resources," but they also showed that such an economy need not be a capitalist economy. They demonstrated that a socialist economy, in which the means of production were collectively owned, could also operate (through perfect planning or through decentralized decision-making) in a state of "optimal economic efficiency." Private ownership had absolutely no formal or theoretical importance in the neoclassical theory. Furthermore, under socialist ownership, they argued, the inequities of income distribution under a capitalist system would disappear.

[31] Ibid., pp. 16–17.

[32] Monsen, op. cit., p. 45.

[33] Larson, op. cit., p. 17.

[34] Oscar Lange and Fred M. Taylor, *On the Economic Theory of Socialism* (Minneapolis, Minn.: University of Minnesota Press, 1938). Lange had published his essay two years earlier in *Review of Economic Studies* (October 1936), pp. 53–71, and (February 1937), pp. 123–142.

The conclusion that many people drew from this book was that the neoclassical liberal ideology could be used equally as well (if not better) as an ideology of socialism. This was, indeed, a radical undermining of neoclassical economics as an ideology defending capitalism.

The classical liberal ideology was rejected by many persons, however, because it seemed to present a severely distorted picture of the realities of twentieth-century capitalism. Its basic assumption of pure competition, that no buyers or sellers were large enough to affect prices, was patently ridiculous. Furthermore, it had little or nothing to say about the important problem of pollution of the environment. Economists also established that the simple counter-cyclical policies in the "neoclassical-Keynesian synthesis" were insufficient to obviate the problems of capitalism's cyclical instability.[35]

Finally, the coup de grace came in J. De V. Graaff's tightly reasoned *Theoretical Welfare Economics*.[36] Graaff showed that economists had not really appreciated the long and restrictive list of assumptions necessary for the optimally efficient allocation of resources envisioned in the model of a competitive, free-market capitalism to be realized. He cited 17 such assumptions,[37] many of which were so restrictive and unrealistic that Graaff concluded that "the measure of acceptance . . . [this theory] has won among professional economists would be astonishing were not its pedigree so long and respectable."[38]

A few of Graaff's 17 conditions will suffice to illustrate his point. Neoclassical ideology requires (1) that any individual's welfare is identical with his preference-ordering, that is, that children, dope addicts, fiends, criminals, and lunatics, as well as all other persons, always prefer that which is best for them; (2) that neither risk nor uncertainty is ever present; (3) that productivity is totally unaffected by the existing distribution of wealth; and (4) that all capital goods, as well as consumer goods, are infinitely divisible. In the opinion of many, this book completely destroyed the basis for the economic analysis upon which the classical liberal ideology was constructed.

[35] On this last point, see Milton Friedman, "The Effects of a Full Employment Policy on Economic Stability: A Formal Analysis," in *Essays in Positive Economics* (Chicago: University of Chicago Press, 1953); and William J. Baumol, "Pitfalls in Counter-Cyclical Policies: Some Tools and Results," *The Review of Economics and Statistics* (February 1961), pp. 21–26.

[36] J. De V. Graaff, *Theoretical Welfare Economics* (London: Cambridge University Press, 1967).

[37] Ibid., pp. 142–154.

[38] Ibid., p. 142.

CRITICISMS OF THE MANAGERIAL IDEOLOGY

The managerial ideology has also come under extensive criticism. Many economists (including several in the neoclassical tradition) argue that bigness on the scale of American big business cannot be shown to be related to efficiency or better service. Giant corporations are presently much larger than maximum productive efficiency would dictate. These economists contend that a drastic reduction in the size of many corporate giants would greatly increase productive efficiency.[39] Examples such as the electric power industry's competition with the Tennessee Valley Authority (TVA), the oligopolistic airlines' struggle with small, unscheduled competitors, and the challenge to the American steel industry from foreign competition are used to point out that private profits and monopoly power, not social welfare or social efficiency, are the prime motivations of big business.[40]

Critics also argue that managers have exactly the same motives as owner-capitalists. They cite an extensive study of the behavior of "management-controlled" and "owner-controlled" giant corporations, which showed that managers were as profit-oriented as owner-capitalists. The author of the study concluded that "it would appear that the proponents of theories of managerial discretion have expended considerable time and effort in describing a phenomenon of relatively minor importance. The large management-controlled corporations seem to be just about as profit-oriented as the large owner-controlled corporations."[41]

Many critics assert that modern managers have no more social conscience or "soul" than the nineteenth-century robber barons. The late Professor Edwin H. Sutherland, once known as the "dean of American criminologists" and former president of the American Sociological Association, conducted a thorough and scholarly investigation of the extent to which corporate executives were involved in criminal behavior. He took the 70 largest nonfinancial corporations, made only a few additions and deletions (due to special circumstances), and traced their criminal histories through official records.[42] There were 980 court decisions against these corporations. One corporation had 50 decisions against it, and the average per

39 See, for example, Walter Adams, "Competition, Monopoly, and Planning," in M. Zeitlin, ed., *American Society, Inc.* (Chicago: Markham, 1970), pp. 240–248.

40 Ibid.

41 Robert J. Larner, "The Effect of Management-Control on the Profits of Larger Corporations," in Zeitlin, op. cit., p. 258.

42 Edwin H. Sutherland, *White Collar Crime* (New York: Holt, Rinehart & Winston, 1961).

corporation was 14. Sixty of the corporations had been found guilty of restraining trade; 53, of infringements; 44, of unfair labor practices; 28, of misrepresentation in advertising; 26, of giving illegal rebates; and 43, of a variety of other offenses. There were a total of 307 individual cases of illegal restraint of trade, 97 of illegal misrepresentation, 222 of infringement, 158 of unfair labor practices, 66 of illegal rebates, and 130 of other offenses.[43] Not all those cases were explicit criminal cases. But 60 percent of the corporations had been found guilty of criminal offenses an average of four times each.

From May 10, 1950, to May 1, 1951, a United States Senate Special Committee to Investigate Crime in Interstate Commerce, under the chairmanship of Senator Estes Kefauver, probed the connections of business and organized crime. Senator Kefauver, Democratic vice-presidential candidate in 1956, later wrote a book based on those hearings. Although he emphasized the fact that there was no evidence to link most big corporations with organized crime, he was nevertheless greatly alarmed at the extent of such connections:

> I cannot overemphasize the danger that can lie in the muscling into legitimate fields by hoodlums . . . there was too much evidence before us of unreformed hoodlums gaining control of a legitimate business; then utilizing all his old mob tricks—strong-arm methods, bombs, even murder—to secure advantages over legitimate competition. All too often such competition either ruins legitimate businessmen or drives them into emulating or merging with the gangsters.
>
> The hoodlums are also clever at concealing ownership of their investments in legitimate fields—sometimes . . . through "trustees" and sometimes by bamboozling respectable businessmen into "fronting" for them.[44]

In 1960, Robert Kennedy, who later became Attorney General of the United States, published *The Enemy Within.* He gathered the material for this book while serving as chief counsel of the United States Senate Select Committee on Improper Activities in the Labor or Management Field. Kennedy, like Kefauver, stressed the fact that he was not condemning all or even most businessmen. He wrote that:

> we found that with the present-day emphasis on money and material goods many businessmen were willing to make corrupt "deals" with dishonest union officials in order to gain competitive advantage or to make a few extra dollars. . . . We came across

43 These data are summarized by F. Lundberg in *The Rich and The Super Rich* (New York: Bantam, 1968), pp. 131–132.

44 Estes Kefauver, *Crime in America* (Garden City, N.Y.: Doubleday, 1951), pp. 139–140.

> more than fifty companies and corporations that had acted improperly—and in many cases illegally—in dealings with labor unions . . . in the companies and corporations to which I am referring the improprieties and illegalities were occasioned solely by a desire for monetary gain. Furthermore we found that we could expect very little assistance from management groups. Disturbing as it may sound, more often the business people with whom we came in contact—and this includes some representatives of our largest corporations—were uncooperative.[45]

Kennedy's list of the names of offending companies included many of the largest and most powerful corporations in the United States.

Ferdinand Lundberg has described the extent to which corporate leaders and management receive either very light punishment or no punishment at all when they become involved in improprieties or illegalities. Among the many cases he cites is

> the case of the bribe of $750,000 by four insurance companies that sent Boss Pendergast of Missouri to jail, later to be pardoned by President Truman. . . . It was almost ten years before the insurance companies were convicted. Then they were only fined; no insurance executives went to jail.
>
> There was, too, the case of Federal Judge Martin Manton who was convicted of accepting a bribe of $250,000 from agents of the defendant when he presided over a case charging exorbitant salaries were improperly paid to officers of the American Tobacco Company. While the attorney for the company was disbarred from federal courts, the assistant to the company president (who made the arrangements) was soon thereafter promoted to vice president: a good boy.[46]

Critics of the managerial ideology do not cite such studies and examples to show businessmen to be criminals. Obviously, most of them are not. The point they wish to make is that the power of monetary incentives and the quest for profits are no less pronounced among managers than among owner-capitalists. In fact, the pressure to acquire ever-increasing profits is so strong on many businessmen and managers that some persistently resort to illegal or improper means. With such pressures, the critics argue, society can ill afford to turn to the managerial class for paternal stewardship of the social and economic welfare.

[45] Robert Kennedy, *The Enemy Within* (New York: Harper & Row, 1960), p. 216.

[46] Lundberg, op. cit., p. 135.

summary

Since World War II, the concentration of corporate power has become more extreme, and inequalities of income distribution have been reduced very little, if at all. Despite these facts, many contemporary ideologies continue to rely on the classical liberal defense of capitalism. Other ideologists continue to place the corporate ethic at the base of their defense of capitalism. This latter group stresses the "efficient, far-sighted policies" of the large corporations, and the "professionalism," as well as "broad, humanistic concerns," of corporate managers. Critics of this point of view argue that the corporate managers are motivated by the same force that moved nineteenth-century capitalists: the quest for maximum profits.

chapter 12 contemporary american capitalism and its radical critics

Radical criticism of American capitalism was widespread during the depression of the 1930s. During the late forties and early fifties, however, pervasive repression of dissent, combined with a relatively prosperous economy, effectively stifled most radical criticism.[1]

All this changed abruptly in the 1960s and early 1970s. The two most important galvanizers of this resurgence of radical criticism were the civil rights movement and the war in Vietnam.

the civil rights movement

The struggle for equality for blacks in America really began in 1619 when the first black slaves were brought to the colonies. Since that time, the struggle has been nearly continuous. In the 1950s, however, the blacks' quest for their basic human rights entered a new phase.

On May 17, 1954, in the case of *Brown* v. *Board of Education of Topeka,* the U.S. Supreme Court unanimously concluded "that in the field of public education the doctrine of 'separate but equal' has no place!" and declared that "separate educational facilities are inherently unequal."

1 For a thorough description of the repression of this period, see Fred J. Cook, *The Nightmare Decade: The Life and Times of Senator Joe McCarthy* (New York: Random House, 1971).

In 1954 and 1955, the few black individuals who applied for admission to white schools were rebuffed and very often suffered severe reprisals. It began to appear that the court decision would have little effect on the patterns of segregation that then existed. In December 1955, however, a black woman in Montgomery, Alabama, refused to give up her bus seat to a white man. She was immediately arrested. Within days, the blacks of Montgomery had organized a boycott of the bus company.

After one year of intense and bitter conflict, the protest ended in victory. The 50,000 blacks of Montgomery succeeded in getting the local bus segregation law nullified. This victory had a symbolic significance that was far greater than the particular issue of bus segregation. Blacks everywhere vicariously shared a new sense of dignity, freedom, and power. They began to organize actively to fight white racism.

Their attempts met with fanatical resistance. In the fall of 1957, Arkansas Governor Orville Faubus used armed troops to bar the entrance of nine black students into Central High School in Little Rock. The federal government interpreted this as a blatant challenge to its authority and sent in paratroopers to enforce the federal court orders. Many southern communities chose to close their public schools rather than allow them to be integrated.

In 1957 and 1960, Congress passed civil rights acts designed to extend voting rights to blacks. The Kennedy Administration urged young people, black and white, to concentrate on a massive registration drive to get southern blacks on the voting lists. Attracting both radical critics of capitalism and liberal young people who generally did not seriously question the basic social and economic system of capitalism, the civil rights movement was nationwide. In the early 1960s, the liberals dominated the movement numerically. They believed that a massive protest against racism would open the public's eyes and that an aroused population would demand new laws which would improve, if not completely cure, the situation.

During this period, civil rights activists organized sit-ins at segregated lunch counters and bus depots, pray-ins at segregated churches, and wade-ins at segregated beaches. Massive, nonviolent demonstrations, or nonviolent civil disobedience, they hoped, would reach the consciences of enough people to achieve integration.

Despite some successes in terms of new civil rights legislation, disillusionment began to affect large numbers of blacks as well as white civil rights workers. They began to realize that political franchisement had little effect on the vast economic inequalities that blacks suffered. Of what use was the vote if a black man could not secure a job, or if he was paid a salary that kept his family in a condition of poverty and degradation? Whereas in 1950, the average salary earned by a black was 61 percent of that earned by a white, by 1962, it had fallen to 55 percent. In the face of a massive civil rights movement, the relative economic position of the blacks had actually deteriorated. Furthermore, whereas in 1950, the rate of unemployment among blacks had been slightly less than twice as high as that for whites, by 1964, it was significantly greater than twice as high. In 1947, blacks constituted 18 percent of the poorest class in America; by 1962, they comprised 22 percent of this class.

Many civil rights advocates became convinced that the most significant barriers to black equality were economic. They turned their attention to a critical analysis of American capitalism as a means of understanding the perpetuation, and indeed the worsening, of the inequities suffered by blacks.

the war in vietnam

The other major force that helped spark the resurgence of radical criticism was the war in Vietnam. Throughout the 1950s, the United States government consistently fought against fundamental social and political change in underdeveloped countries. Under the guise of "protecting the world from communism," the United States had intervened in the internal affairs of at least a score of countries. In some, such as Guatemala and Iran, U.S. agents actually engineered the overthrow of the legitimate governments and replaced them with regimes more to American liking.[2]

Most criticism was muted by the political repression of McCarthyism. The college students of the 1950s, the "silent generation," generally acquiesced in the national mood of anticommunism that provided the justification for political repression at home and extensive intervention in other nations' internal affairs. During the 1950s, American intervention in Vietnam attracted little special attention. It was merely one of many countries that were being "saved from communism." In the 1960s, however, all this was to change drastically. The Vietnam War then became a powerful force in regenerating radical criticism of American capitalism. For this reason, a brief examination of the origins of the Vietnam War is needed here.

During the World War II occupation of Vietnam, the French colonial regime collaborated with the Japanese. Toward the end of the war, the Japanese locked up the colonial administrators and established

[2] For a popular account of these interventions, see David Wise and Thomas B. Ross, *The Invisible Government* (New York: Random House, 1964).

a puppet regime under the Annamite Emperor Bao Dai. Throughout this period, the Americans (and, indeed, all the Allies) had supported a resistance movement (the Vietminh) headed by Ho Chi Minh. When Japan surrendered, there was a peaceful transfer of political power to the Vietminh.

The French did not want to lose this part of their colonial empire but realized that they were too weak to inflict a quick military defeat on the new government. On March 6, 1946, they signed an agreement with the Ho Chi Minh government that read in part: "The government of France recognizes the Republic of Vietnam as a free state having its government and its parliament, its army and its finances, forming part of the Indo-Chinese federation and of the French Union."[3] This agreement clearly intended that the Ho Chi Minh government would enjoy a status similar to the governments of the members of the British Commonwealth. It legally established Ho Chi Minh's regime as the legitimate government of *all* Vietnam. Nothing that subsequently occurred changed this essential fact.

The French were confident, however, that they could make a subservient puppet of Ho Chi Minh. They failed completely in this task. Unable to reduce Ho Chi Minh to this role, they brought back Emperor Bao Dai, even though he had voluntarily abdicated his throne, changed his name, and retired to Hong Kong. They "installed" him as "chief of state" and declared the Vietminh to be outlaws. There followed six years of intensive, bitter warfare. Finally, in 1954, the Vietminh decisively defeated the French. The Geneva Accords (July 1954), which arranged for the French surrender, called for a cease-fire and a *temporary* separating of opposing forces. Ho Chi Minh's followers were to move north of the seventeenth parallel and Emperor Bao Dai's were to move to the south. This arrangement was to end within two years with a national election to choose the leader of all Vietnam. Shortly after these negotiations, American-backed Ngo Dinh Diem ousted Bao Dai, proclaimed the existence of a "Republic of Vietnam," and appointed himself as its first president.

There were no elections. The Americans and Diem simply asserted that now there were two Vietnams. The reason for refusing to have the election was candidly admitted by President Eisenhower in his book *Mandate for Change.*

> I am convinced that the French could not win the war because the internal political situation in Vietnam, weak and confused, badly weakened their military position. I have never talked or corresponded with a person knowledgeable in Indochinese affairs who did not agree that had elections been held as of the time of the fighting, possibly 80

[3] Quoted in Leo Huberman and Paul M. Sweezy, "The Road to Ruin," *Monthly Review* (April 1965), p. 787.

> percent of the population would have voted for Communist Ho Chi Minh as their leader rather than chief of state, Bao Dai.[4]

Obviously, the substitution of Diem for Bao Dai did not change the situation.

This American-imposed solution was rejected not only by Ho Chi Minh and his followers in the North but also by people in the South. So the war of national liberation, which had been fought against the Japanese and the French, was continued against the United States.

Americans were repeatedly told that their government was fighting a war to protect the South Vietnamese from the armed aggression of North Vietnam. The North Vietnamese were pictured as violators of the Geneva agreements, determined to enslave the South Vietnamese.

Critics of American policy challenged this official version of the nature of the war. Their assessment of what was happening in Vietnam received widespread support in academic circles, and college campuses became centers of antiwar sentiment. From the early 1960s through about 1966, most opposition to the war was largely confined to the campuses. During the last years of the decade, however, persons from all segments of society actively opposed the war. The antiwar movement had become a mass movement.

Finally, in 1968, U.S. Secretary of Defense Robert S. McNamara, himself becoming disillusioned with the official rationale for the war, ordered the U.S. Department of Defense to prepare an in-depth account of how the United States became involved. In early 1971, the report was completed. The 7,000-page document was obtained by the *New York Times* which paid researchers to determine whether new facts had been brought to light. The Defense Department admitted that (1) the Eisenhower Administration had played a "direct role in the ultimate breakdown of the Geneva settlement;"[5] (2) from 1954 onward, the United States had engaged in "acts of sabotage and terror warfare against North Vietnam;"[6] (3) the United States "encouraged and abetted the overthrow of President Ngo Dinh Diem" when he was no longer considered to be of use; (4) for many years prior to 1965, the United States government undertook "the careful preparation of public opinion for the years of open warfare that were to follow."[7]

American involvement increased steadily until by 1968, the United States had an army of over 500,000 men on Vietnamese soil and were spending nearly $3 billion per month ($100 million per day!)

4 Quoted in ibid., p. 789.

5 Quoted in Neil Sheehan, "The Story Behind the Vietnam War, Based on a Pentagon Study," *New York Times News Service,* June 13, 1971.

6 Ibid.

7 Ibid.

attempting to impose a "suitable political solution" on the Vietnamese.[8]

As American battle casualties rose (hundreds of thousands of Americans have been wounded and well over 50,000 Americans have been killed), young people everywhere began to question the morality of the war. Beginning in 1964, teach-ins protesting the war were mounted on college campuses around the United States. Most organizers and participants were convinced that American involvement in the war was a tragic mistake that would be rectified if the public could be made aware of the true facts of the situation.

The antiwar movement grew rapidly. President Johnson's landslide victory in 1964, as well as his decision not to seek another term in 1968, are often attributed in part at least to the powerful, widespread opposition to the war. After a few years of debate, however, antiwar critics were convinced that most Americans did know the basic facts of Vietnam and wanted a hasty end to the war. Yet the American government, without giving any convincing reasons for its actions, continued to seek military victory.

Critics began to ask whether there was not some deeper motive than simple anticommunist sentiment propelling the American government. In particular, they began to search for an economic motive or an economic rationale for the war. They began seriously to reexamine the older radical theories of capitalist imperialism.

contemporary critiques of american capitalism

The frustrations of the civil rights movement and the antiwar movement led to a burgeoning literature critical of the basic institutions of American capitalism. As had earlier critiques, this literature censured the grossly unequal distribution of income, wealth, and power in the United States. These critics, as did the left-Keynesians, deplored the extent to which post–World War II economic stability had been purchased at a cost of thoroughgoing militarism (discussed in Chapters 10 and 11).

On these points, radical and liberal critics have been in agreement. Liberal critics believe that political reform and electoral politics are sufficient to correct these perversions of the American economy. Radical critics, however, believe that inequality and militarism are inherent to a capitalist economy, and that it also necessarily involves

[8] As of this writing (December 1971), there is no end in sight in the Vietnam War, despite the fact that the American army has succeeded in training more Vietnamese to do the fighting, and hence has been able to reduce American troop strength. The destruction of Vietnam through air attacks has, in fact, intensified.

(1) imperialistic exploitation of underdeveloped countries as a means of maintaining high output and large profits in the United States, (2) endemic discrimination against minority groups and women, (3) inability to control pollution and exhaustion of resources and (4) a degrading commercialism and social alienation. In the remainder of this chapter, some of the literature in these four general areas will be described.

american imperialism

One of the first and most influential of these critics was Paul A. Baran. His book *The Political Economy of Growth,*[9] first published in 1957, has undergone two editions, has been translated into several languages, and has sold very well in the United States and even better in most underdeveloped countries. Baran argued that before an underdeveloped country could industrialize, it would have to mobilize its *economic surplus,* or the difference between what is produced and what has to be consumed in order to maintain the economy's productivity. It is the source of investment capital with which the country can industrialize. Under present institutional arrangements, most underdeveloped countries either waste their surpluses or lose them to imperialistic capitalist countries.

"Far from serving as an engine of economic expansion, of technological progress and of social change, the capitalist order in . . . [underdeveloped] countries has represented a framework for economic stagnation, for archaic technology, and for social backwardness."[10] The peasant agriculture usually produces a sufficiently large surplus in these countries. In fact, Baran pointed out the surplus is frequently as high as 50 percent of the total amount produced. "The subsistence peasants' obligations on account of rent, taxes, and interest in all underdeveloped countries are very high. They frequently absorb more than half of his meager net product."[11]

The problem is in the disposition of this surplus. Part goes to middlemen, speculators, moneylenders, and merchants—petty capitalists who have neither the interest nor the wherewithal to finance industrialization. A much larger part goes to the landowning ruling class which uses its "share" to purchase luxury consumption goods, usually imported from capitalist countries, and the extensive military establishments needed to maintain their internal power.

9 Paul A. Baran, *The Political Economy of Growth* (New York: Monthly Review Press, 1962).

10 Ibid., pp. 163–164.

11 Ibid., p. 165.

Importing luxuries and military hardware necessitates sending exports to the industrialized countries. Exports usually consist of one or two primary agricultural products or mineral resources. The capitalist countries with which they trade have such monopsonistic buying power that the terms of trade are very unfavorable to the underdeveloped countries. The large, multinational corporations that purchase the raw materials are not interested in the industrialization of these countries. Thus, foreign capitalist investment is limited to that which is necessary for the profitable extraction of resources.

An alliance between reactionary land owning class and foreign capitalists protects both their interests by suppressing dissidence and keeping the masses at a subsistence standard of living. Thus, landowners can maintain their position and capitalists are guaranteed cheap labor and large profits.

> Small wonder that under such circumstances Western big business heavily engaged in raw materials exploitation leaves no stone unturned to obstruct the evolution of social and political conditions in underdeveloped countries that might be conducive to their economic development. It uses its tremendous power to prop up the backward areas' comprador administrations, to disrupt and corrupt the social and political movements that oppose them, and to overthrow whatever progressive governments may rise to power and refuse to do the bidding of their imperialistic overlords.[12]

Baran believed that the American government works hand in hand with American big business. Most U.S. economic and military aid provided underdeveloped countries is given, in his opinion, in order to prop up client governments.

Often such governments are not strong enough to survive on their own, even with this aid. Under these circumstances, the United States intervenes, either clandestinely (through CIA sabotage and intrigue) or directly (through the use of military force).

Baran and like-minded critics see the interventions in Guatemala, Iran, Korea, Cuba, the Dominican Republic, Vietnam, and Cambodia as examples of American endeavors to protect business interests, both current and potential, against threats from more progressive social and political movements. They point to 53 different "U.S. defense commitments and assurances" that commit the United States to the use of military force to maintain existing governments, very often against their own people.[13]

The dependence of underdeveloped countries upon a small number of export commodities is documented in a study based on

12 Ibid., p. 198.

13 See Harry Magdoff, *The Age of Imperialism, The Economics of U.S. Foreign Policy* (New York: Monthly Review Press, Modern Reader Paperbacks, 1969), pp. 203–206.

International Monetary Fund data. Each of the 37 countries considered earns 58 to 99 percent of its export receipts from 1 to 6 commodities.[14] Furthermore, the United States depends upon imports as the principal source for most of the 62 types of materials the Defense Department classifies as "strategic and critical." For 38 of these, 80 to 100 percent of the new supplies are imported; for 14 more, 40 to 79 percent are imported.[15]

A large and increasing percentage of U.S. corporate sales and profits results from exports and sales of foreign subsidiaries (many of which, of course, are in underdeveloped countries).[16] Furthermore, detailed examination reveals that the foreign trade of the underdeveloped countries is very lopsided. Raw materials and metals in their first state of smelting constitute 85 percent of exports; manufactured goods (mostly textiles), only 10 percent. But about 60 percent of their imports are manufactured goods.[17] Because most manufactured imports are consumer goods, such a pattern of trade cannot lead to development, but only to continued economic dependence.

Critics of this point of view (i.e., defenders of American economic foreign policy) argue that although foreign trade and foreign investments are important to American corporations, they also benefit the underdeveloped countries. The orthodox argument is expressed in a widely used textbook:

> In general, a restrained optimism as to the future prospects for underdeveloped countries in their trading relations with the developed countries seems to be warranted. The most encouraging sign is the growing recognition on the part of developed countries that opening their markets to the export products of underdeveloped areas is an essential part of their accepted program to assist underdeveloped countries to grow.[18]

But this position does not deal directly with radical critiques of American economic foreign policy. It simply assumes that all the underdeveloped countries need is *more* trade. Another orthodox scholar who studied the problem more thoroughly admits that "increasing the flow of private capital to underdeveloped countries will probably require a *recasting of economic policies* in both underdeveloped and advanced countries."[19] He does not go on to

14 Magdoff, op. cit., pp. 99–100.

15 Percy W. Bidwell, *Raw Materials* (New York: Harper & Row, 1958), p. 12.

16 Magdoff, op. cit., p. 57.

17 Pierre Jalee, *The Pillage of the Third World* (New York: Monthly Review Press, 1965), p. 8.

18 Delbert A. Snider, *Introduction to International Economics* (Homewood, Ill.: Irwin, 1963), p. 548.

19 Benjamin Higgins, *Economic Development* (New York: Norton, 1959), p. 593; italics added.

analyze what obstacles prevent this "recasting of economic policies."

Conservative defenders of American policies grant that developed capitalist countries have had immense economic, political, and military power which they have used to influence and control peoples around the world. They deny, however, that this "imperialism" is basically economic in nature. Thus, the widely respected economic historian Professor David S. Landes writes:

> It seems to me that one has to look at imperialism as a multifarious response to a common opportunity that consists simply in disparity of power. Whenever and wherever such disparity has existed, people and groups have been ready to take advantage of it. It is, one notes with regret, in the nature of the human beast to push other people around—or to save their souls or "civilize" them as the case may be.[20]

One radical critic has answered this assertion by noting that the modern capitalist drive to save people's souls from communism and to civilize them is perfectly compatible with economic motives. He cites the following quotation from an officer of General Electric Company: "Thus, our search for profits places us squarely in line with the national policy of stepping up international trade as a means of strengthening the free world in the Cold War confrontation with Communism." The critic, Harry Magdoff, summarizes his position: "Just as the fight against Communism helps the search for profits, so the search for profits helps the fight against Communism. What more perfect harmony of interests could be imagined?"[21]

Many books written in the 1960s attempted to explain contemporary American foreign policy—and the cold war between the United States and the Soviet Union—in terms of American economic imperialism.[22]

racism and sexism

Radical critics also point to the pervasive effects of discrimination based upon race and sex that exists in capitalist countries, particularly in the United States. Virtually everyone agrees that racism and sexism create severe discrimination. Defenders of American capitalism explain this discrimination in one of two ways.

[20] David S. Landes, "The Nature of Economic Imperialism," *The Journal of Economic History* (December 1961), p. 510.

[21] Magdoff, op. cit., pp. 200–201.

[22] See Magdoff, op. cit., D. F. Fleming, *The Cold War and Its Origins* (Garden City, N.Y.: Doubleday, 1961); Gar Alperowitz, *Atomic Diplomacy: Hiroshima and Potsdam* (New York: Simon & Schuster, 1965); David Horowitz, ed., *Corporations and the Cold War* (New York: Monthly Review Press, 1969); and David Horowitz, *Empire and Revolution* (New York: Random House, 1969).

The more reactionary is to argue that job discrimination merely reflects the innate inferiority of women and blacks. Few, if any, intellectuals embrace this position, but it apparently is accepted by a large minority in the United States. The other contention is that racism and sexism are products of a fairly universal human bigotry and are not related to capitalism or any other economic system.

Critics of capitalism point out that the wages of blacks and women make up a significant part of capitalists' wage costs. In 1969, for example, the wages of American women averaged only about 60 percent of the wages of men doing the same jobs. On that basis, it would appear that approximately 23 percent of all manufacturing profits are attributable to the lower wages paid to women. Profits made as a result of racial discrimination would certainly be smaller, but they would still be significant.

In one of the most influential socialist critiques, Paul A. Baran and Paul M. Sweezy have argued that it is necessary to

> Consider first the private interests which benefit from the existence of a Negro subproletariat. (a) Employers benefit from divisions in the labor force which enable them to play one group off against another, thus weakening all. . . . (b) Owners of ghetto real estate are able to overcrowd and overcharge. (c) Middle and upper income groups benefit from having at their disposal a large supply of cheap domestic labor. (d) Many small marginal businesses, especially in the service trades, can operate profitably only if cheap labor is available to them. (e) White workers benefit by being protected from Negro competition for the more desirable and higher paying jobs.[23]

They also assert that in addition to increasing profits, discrimination increases social stability in a capitalist economy. The class structure of capitalism, they hold, leads to a situation in which

> each status group has a deep-rooted psychological need to compensate for feelings of inferiority and envy toward those above by feelings of superiority and contempt for those below. It thus happens that a special pariah group at the bottom acts as a kind of lightening rod for the frustrations and hostilities of all the higher groups, the more so the nearer they are to the bottom. It may even be said that the very existence of the pariah group is a kind of harmonizer and stabilizer of the social structure.[24]

Although Baran and Sweezy's assertions pertain to racism, many critics argue that sexism performs much the same function in a

[23] Paul A. Baran and Paul M. Sweezy, *Monopoly Capital* (New York: Monthly Review Press, 1966), pp. 263–264.

[24] Ibid., pp. 265–266.

capitalist society. These critics generally do not believe that capitalism is the original creator of racism and sexism, but rather that capitalism perpetuates and intensifies racism and sexism because they serve valuable functions.

> Today, transferring the locus of whites' perceptions of the source of many of their problems from capitalism and toward blacks, racism continues to serve the needs of the capitalist system. Although an individual employer might gain by refusing to discriminate and agreeing to hire blacks at above the going black wage rate, it is not true that the capitalist class as a whole would profit if racism were eliminated and labor were more efficiently allocated without regard to skin color. . . . The divisiveness of racism weakens workers' strength when bargaining with employers; the economic consequences of racism are not only lower incomes for blacks but also higher incomes for the capitalist class coupled with lower incomes for white workers. Although capitalists may not have conspired consciously to create racism, and although capitalists may not be its principal perpetuators, nevertheless racism does support the continued well-being of the American capitalist system.[25]

alienation

Many contemporary radical critics have refined and elaborated upon Marx's theory of the human alienation inherent in the capitalist economic system.[26] Baran and Sweezy, for example, maintain that total alienation pervades and dominates contemporary American capitalism:

> Disorientation, apathy, and often despair, haunting Americans in all walks of life, have assumed in our time the dimensions of a prolonged crisis. This crisis affects every aspect of national life, and ravages both its socio-political and its individual spheres—everyman's everyday existence. A heavy strangulating sense of the emptiness and futility of life permeates the country's moral and intellectual climate. High level committees are entrusted with the discovery and specification of "national goals" while gloom pervades the printed matter (fiction and non-fiction, alike) appearing daily in the literary market place. The malaise deprives work of meaning and purpose; turns leisure into joyless, debilitating laziness; fatally

[25] Michael Reich, "The Economics of Racism," in David M. Gordon, ed., *Problems in Political Economy: An Urban Perspective* (Lexington, Mass.: Raytheon/Heath, 1971), pp. 109–110.

[26] See Chapter 6.

> impairs the education system and the conditions of healthy growth in the young; transforms religion and church into commercialized vehicles of "togetherness"; and destroys the very foundation of burgeois society, the family.[27]

The fact of alienation, like the facts of racism and sexism, is explained by many defenders of capitalism as an unfortunate but inevitable by-product of industrial civilization. An industrialized socialist economy would, they assert, create the same type of alienation. Few people, regardless of political and economic views, would be willing to forego the advantages of industrialization in order to combat alienation. And even if people did want to return to preindustrial society, there is simply no practical way of turning back time to some imagined golden age.

Socialist critics reply that although some amount of alienation will surely exist in any industrialized society, capitalism significantly intensifies alienation and makes it more pervasive. Erich Fromm, the famous psychoanalyst, social philosopher, and author, argues that the most important single cause of alienation is the fact that the individual feels no sense of participation in the forces that determine social policy. He sees these forces as anonymous and totally beyond the sphere of any individual's influence. "The anonymity of the social forces," writes Fromm, "is inherent in the structure of the capitalist mode of production."[28]

Fromm identifies several types of alienation created by the capitalist mode of production. Conditions of employment alienate workers. Their livelihoods depend upon whether capitalists and managers are able to make a profit by hiring them, and thus they are viewed as means only, never as ends. The individual worker is "an economic atom that dances to the tune of atomistic management." Managers "strip the worker of his right to think and move freely. Life is being denied; need to control, creativeness, curiosity, and independent thought are being balked, and the result, the inevitable result, is flight or fight on the part of the worker, apathy or destructiveness, psychic regression.[29]

And yet Fromm argues that the "role of the manager is also one of alienation," for he too is coerced by the ineluctable forces of capitalism and has very little freedom. He must deal "with impersonal giants; with the giant competitive enterprise; with giant impersonal markets; with giant unions, and the giant government."[30] His position,

[27] Baran and Sweezy, op. cit., p. 281.

[28] Erich Fromm, *The Sane Society* (New York: Fawcett World Library, Premier Books, 1965), p. 125.

[29] Quoted in ibid., p. 115.

[30] Ibid., pp. 115–116.

his status, his income, in short, his very social existence, all depend upon making ever-increasing amounts of profits. Yet he must do this in a world in which he has little personal influence upon the giants with whom he deals.

Fromm also maintains that the process of consumption in a capitalist society "is as alienated as the process of production." The truly human way of acquiring commodities, according to Fromm, would be through need and the desire to use: "The acquisition of bread and clothing [should] depend on no other premise than that of being alive; the acquisition of books and paintings on my effort to understand them and my ability to use them."[31] But in capitalist societies, the income with which to purchase these commodities can only come through sales in the impersonal market.

As a consequence, those who have money are subjected to a constant barrage of propaganda designed to create consuming automata. Capitalist socialization processes make consumption-hungry, irrational, compulsive buying machines of us all. The acts of buying and consuming have become ends in themselves, with little or no relation to the uses or pleasures derived from the commodities.

> Man today is fascinated by the possibility of buying more, better, and especially, new things. He is consumption-hungry. The act of buying and consuming has become a compulsive, irrational aim, because it is an end in itself, with little relation to the use of or pleasure in the things bought and consumed. To buy the latest gadget, the latest model of anything that is on the market, is the dream of everybody in comparison to which the real pleasure in use is quite secondary. Modern man, if he dared to be articulate about his concept of heaven, would describe a vision which would look like the biggest department store in the world, showing new things and gadgets, and himself having plenty of money with which to buy them. He would wander around open-mouthed in his heaven of gadgets and commodities, provided only that there were ever more and newer things to buy, and perhaps that his neighbors were just a little less privileged than he.[32]

Finally, the most severe alienation is the alienation of a man from his "self." A person's "worth" in a capitalist market economy is determined in the same way as the "worth" of anything else: by sales in the marketplace. In this situation,

> man experiences himself as a thing to be employed successfully on the market. He does not experience himself as an active agent, as the bearer of human powers. He is alienated from these powers. His

[31] Ibid., p. 120.

[32] Ibid., p. 123.

> aim is to sell himself successfully on the market. His sense of self does not stem from his activity as a loving and thinking individual, but from his socio-economic role. . . . If you ask a man "Who are you?", he answers "I am a manufacturer," "I am a clerk," "I am a doctor." . . . That is the way he experiences himself, not as a man, with love, fear, convictions, doubts, but as that abstraction, alienated from his real nature, which fulfills a certain function in the social system. His sense of value depends on his success: on whether he can sell himself favorably, whether he can make more of himself than he started out with, whether he is a success. His body, his mind and his soul are his capital, and his task in life is to invest it favorably, to make a *profit* of himself. Human qualities like friendliness, courtesy, kindness, are transformed into commodities, into assets of the "personality package," conducive to a higher price on the personality market. If the individual fails in a profitable investment of himself, *he* feels that he is a failure; if he succeeds, he is a success. Clearly, his sense of his own value always depends on factors extraneous to himself, on the fickle judgment of the market, which decides about his value as it decides about the value of commodities. He, like all commodities that cannot be sold profitably on the market, is worthless as far as his exchange value is concerned, even though his use value may be considerable.[33]

Thus, socialist critics argue that the impersonal nexus of the capitalist market mediates all human relationships. It makes profit and loss the ultimate and pervasive evaluative criteria of human worth. This means that human alienation must inevitably be extremely severe in a capitalist market economy.

environmental destruction

Capitalism must either experience economic growth or suffer depression, unemployment, stagnation, and all the attendent social problems (see Chapter 10 for a discussion of the reasons). But economic growth can also create situations in which the pursuit of profits comes into direct conflict with the public welfare. Critics of capitalism have argued that corporate profit-seeking is generally accompanied by very little concern for conservation or for a clean, livable environment.

Pollution is of concern to defenders of capitalism as well as to critics. Defenders argue that it is a problem common to all industrialized economies. Critics assert that the problem is worse in

[33] Ibid., pp. 129–130.

a capitalist economy. Furthermore, they maintain that it would be virtually impossible to control pollution effectively in a capitalist system. This is so, they argue, because the basic economic cause of pollution in a capitalist economy is that business firms do not have to pay for *all* the costs incurred in the production process. They pay for labor, raw materials, and capital used up in production. But they use the land, air, and water for the disposal of waste products that are created in the process of production. Generally, they pay little or nothing for the use of the environment as a garbage disposal.

It has been estimated[34] that each year businesses are responsible for over 25 billion tons of pollutants being spewed in the air and dumped into the water and on the land. This is about 125 tons of waste per year for every man, woman, and child in the United States. Included in this figure are about 150 million tons of smoke and fumes that blacken the skies and poison the air, 22 million tons of waste paper products, 3 million tons of milltailings, and 50 trillion gallons of heated and polluted liquids that are dumped into streams, rivers, and lakes each year.

Critics argue that it is extremely difficult if not impossible for a capitalist economy to deal with these problems because those who receive the profits from production do not pay these social costs, and those who do pay the social costs have little or no voice in the operation of the businesses.

In response to the widespread public demand for control of pollution and polluters, the government has given contracts to many corporations to devise new methods of combating pollution. In effect, the government is asking private corporations to act as the controllers of other private corporations. Radical critics are convinced that this corporate integration of polluters and controllers will never lead to any substantial improvement. Most of the important pollution-control companies have become subsidiaries of the giant corporations that do most of the polluting.

One radical critic has analyzed the effects of this corporate control.

> It is the chemical industry . . . that best illustrates the consequences of the incest between the pollution control business and the industrial polluters. First, the chemical industry is in the enviable position of reaping sizable profits by attempting to clean up rivers and lakes (at public expense) which they have profitably polluted in the first place. To facilitate this practically every major chemical company in the U.S. has established a pollution abatement division or is in the process of doing so. . . .

[34] These estimates are taken from an important and impressive study on pollution: R. C. d'Arge, A. V. Kneese, and R. V. Ayres, *Economics of the Environment: A Materials Balance Approach* (Baltimore: Johns Hopkins, 1970).

> A second consequence of placing the "control" of pollution in the hands of big business is that the official abatement levels will inevitably be set low enough to protect industry's power to pollute and therefore its ability to keep costs down and revenues high. According to a recent study by the FWPCA (Federal Water Pollution Control Administration) if the chemical industry were to reduce its pollution of water to zero, the costs involved would amount to almost $2.7 billion per year. This would cut profits almost by half.[35]

Under such circumstances, the critics do not expect much progress in cleaning up the environment unless fundamental social, political, and economic changes occur first.

liberal versus radical critiques of capitalism

The glaringly unequal distribution of wealth, income, and political power and the facts of militarism, imperialism, vicious discrimination, social alienation, and environmental destruction are all recognized and decried by both liberal and radical critics of capitalism. There is, however, an immensely important difference between the positions of liberals and radicals.

Liberals tend to see each of these social and economic problems as separate and distinct. The problems, they believe, are the results of past mistakes, inabilities, and ineptitudes or the results of random cases of individual perversity. Liberals also tend to consider the government as detached, disinterested, and motivated by a desire to maximize the welfare of all its citizens. Hence, liberals generally favor government-sponsored reforms designed to mitigate the many evils of capitalism. These reforms never threaten the two most important features of capitalism: private ownership of the means of production and the free market.

Radicals, however, see each of the social and economic problems we have discussed as the *direct consequence* of private ownership of capital and the process of social decision-making within the impersonal cash nexus of the market. The problems cannot be solved until their underlying causes are eliminated, but this means a fundamental, radical economic reorganization. If private ownership of capital is eliminated, and if significant restrictions are placed on the areas in which the market determines social decisions, the resulting system would no longer be a capitalist economic system. It would, of necessity, be some type of socialist society.

[35] Martin Gellen, "The Making of a Pollution-Industrial Complex," in Gordon, op. cit., pp. 469–470.

summary

From the late 1950s to the early 1970s, the civil rights movement and the antiwar movement generated a resurgence of radical criticism of American capitalism. The radicals argue that inequality, discrimination, alienation, environmental destruction, militarism, and imperialism are integral parts of a capitalist economy. Unlike liberals, who believe that these evils are accidental and that the system can be reformed, radicals contend that these evils cannot be overcome unless the basic structure of capitalism is fundamentally changed.

The principal obstacle to the achievement of such reforms is the fact that political power is derived from economic power. Radicals see capitalist governments as plutocracies hidden behind phony façades of democracy. Both political parties, they point out, spend many millions of dollars on each election. As a consequence, both political parties are almost completely controlled by the wealthiest 2 percent of the population that owns most of the income-producing capital.[36] In this situation, one would not expect the wealthy elite to support any government that threatened to destroy the basis of their wealth, privileges, and power. Therefore, fundamental reform seems unlikely unless a reformist movement can establish a base of power that is independent of wealth. This explains the popularity at radical gatherings of the slogan, "Power to the People!"

[36] For detailed evidence for this point of view, see G. William Domhoff, *Who Rules America* (Englewood Cliffs, N.J.: Prentice-Hall, 1967), and Domhoff, *The Higher Circles: The Governing Class in America* (New York: Random House, 1970).

index

72 73 74 75 76 9 8 7 6 5 4 3 2 1